AMERICAN AID TO ISRAEL:
NATURE AND IMPACT

Including the Uncensored Draft Report of the GAO:
U.S. Assistance to the State of Israel

AMERICAN AID TO ISRAEL:
NATURE AND IMPACT

MOHAMED EL-KHAWAS / SAMIR ABED-RABBO

Foreword by **RABBI ELMER BERGER**

AMANA BOOKS

ISBN 0-915597-03-9

AMANA BOOKS
58 Elliot Street
Brattleboro, Vermont 05301

Designed by Ed Helminski
Printed in the United States of America

I have counted twenty years
arguing with my friend the good American
over a curious object
not far in the distance.
He has maintained it's a goat,
I have persisted a swan.
One day we brought the matter
to a showdown and shot at it
to scare it, not to kill,
and the object rose and flew away,
annoyed but not afraid.
My friend calmly reaffirmed
"A goat, a goat, even though it flies."

Rejae Busailah

CONTENTS

FOREWORD

This analysis of United States economic and military aid to the State of Israel speaks for itself. The problem will be to persuade enough Americans—private citizens and government officials—to read it. Big money is involved, perhaps in the neighborhood of $40 *billion* since 1949. The package contains United States Treasury funds (collected in taxes from United States citizens), "charitable" contributions (tax-deductible dollars), sales of State of Israel Bonds (unlike other foreign securities, exempted by special legislation from the Interest Equalization Tax) and private investments in Israel by both individuals and corporations.

Of the more than $25 billion of United States governmental transfers, more than half are classified as "grants," to be differentiated from "loans."

On November 29, 1983, Reagan promised that for fiscal year 1984, the entire assistance package would be a non-repayable "grant." The figures for the unprecedented handout total $2.61 *billion*. Military assistance to the already most powerful military state in the Middle East and probably the fourth most powerful in the world, will be $1.7 *billion*. "Economic assistance" was set at $910 million. The United States Sixth Fleet, stationed in the Mediterranean, will purchase $200 million worth of supplies from Israel.

The "cooperative" ally's bid for military assistance was $1.7 billion—nearly a half-*billion* more than Reagan's "Big Hearted Herbert" offer.[1] When push comes to shove in an election year, and the appropriation and budget bills are before the Congress, no known political savant was wagering the Israelis would lose.

In June of 1983, the General Accounting Office of the United States Government released a report, *U.S. Assistance to the State of Israel.*[2] Sometime after the official public release, the American-Arab Anti-Discrimination Committee obtained and circulated an "uncensored" draft of the report.[3] The statistical material in the present book's chapter, "U.S. Aid to Israel: An Assessment" is fully supported by both versions of the GAO document. Claudia Wright, Washington Correspondent for London's *New Statesman* and Paris's *Temoignage Chretien,* says:

> The most important revelation in the GAO report is the disdain, even contempt which the Israeli government displays toward officials of the US government agencies with whom they regularly deal, and on whom they materially depend.[4]

Space permits mention here of only a few examples of the information Washington officialdom intended to conceal from the Americans who pay the bills.

In 1982, the haughty, "independent" Zionist state owed the United States $875 million "for debt servicing" alone. "$810 million (93 percent) is for defense loans." But "grace periods" for repayment of previous loans for military purposes are coming to an end. According to the GAO, this means that the Zionist state either will have to use the "cash transfers" it has been receiving as "economic assistance" to repay these maturing debts incurred for military purposes, or the United States will be called upon to increase its so-called "economic assistance" so Israel can maintain an "honorable" credit rating and avoid excessive interest charges at commercial rates.[5] Both of these financial hanky-pankies seem to have been incorporated in the Reagan "freebees," cavalierly offered out of American tax-payers' money. "Economic assistance" has been upped from an average of $785 million per year to the now-proposed $910 million. The semantical difference between "military" and "economic" is pure political window dressing.

The absurdity beggars description. The "rich" creditor "loans" its hard earned money to the profligate debtor so the profligate debtor can pay its debts to the creditor with the creditor's own money. And the victimized American tax-payers are set up to be mystified by the misleading labels! And all this recklessness with the public trust while the creditor's legitimate family—United States citizens—are harassed by $200 billion-a-year deficits in the federal budget, with continued high mortgage rates preventing many members of the family from purchasing needed homes, with the certainty of increased taxation to reduce budget deficits as soon as the next elections are over, with cities and states trembling on the verge of insolvency and reducing citizen-services because of sustained high rates of interest they must pay on their "municipal bond offerings." The Reaganites, exploiting an image of pursuing the old, homely, American virtues have apparently deleted "charity begins at home" from their political almanac.

And for what! For interminable courting of America's "only strong, reliable ally" in the Middle East. But the reports of the November Reagan-Shamir meetings disclose that the "ally" told the "America Great Again" President to "pack that stuff in." Reagan wanted two major concessions from the collaborator in the murder of Count Bernadotte and the opponent of the Egyptian/Israeli treaty. First, Reagan wanted an Israeli agreement to modify the May 17, 1983 "withdrawal" agreement with Lebanon as a way to breathe life into the expiring Reagan peace "process." This modification was designed to accommodate the "reconciliation" conference at which the major warring parties in Lebanon were searching for a formula to eliminate all foreign troops from the country and facilitate an internal settlement to establish a more representative government which would be capable of exercising sovereignty over all Lebanese territory.

The second major concession the Reaganites sought was a "freeze" on further Zionist settlements in the occupied territories—particularly the West Bank and Gaza. The freeze is necessary if Reagan's September 1982 peace "process" is to have a chance of success.

To both of these requests, reflecting American interests, the dedicated anti-communist, committed friend of the United States, gave an emphatic "Nyet!"

The Israelis also objected to any American arms sales to "Arab countries such as Jordan and Saudi Arabia." They requested, and Reagan agreed to, negotiations for a duty-free trade accord to increase Israeli exports and ease its unfavorable trade balance.

Quoting Reagan again, it was agreed to establish:

> [A] joint political-military group to examine ways in which we can enhance Israeli-American cooperation [to challenge] the threat to our mutual interest, posed by increased Soviet involvement in the Middle East.

Hoping the reading audience would see, in its minds-eye one of those pixie, boyish head-nods and other body-English, with a tilt toward truth and a lurch toward the 1984 elections, the "stars and stripes forever" President did admit he and Shamir had "discussed some issues on which we don't see eye-to-eye." Added *The New York Times,* "but he minimized their importance." Of which issues? Putting Lebanon back together again? The interminable search for Israeli "security"? How to persuade an Arab world no longer trusting America to come into negotiations for a comprehensive peace? At the prices the Zionist leaders of our "ally" are charging, don't the American people who pay the bill have a right to know what issues their President considers of minimal importance?

Joseph Harsch of *The Christian Science Monitor* (July 5, 1983, p. 26), even before this latest American door-prize for the Israelis, estimated that "Israel draws somewhere around $10 *billion* a year from the U.S. and its citizens." He continues:

[T]he American taxpayer is paying for Israel's living standard, for its
wars, for its conquests and for those settlements which are going up
throughout the occupied Arab territories . . .

All of these jeopardize long-range American interests, frighten our allies,
who are directly dependent upon Middle East oil, and leave the Soviet
Union to play the waiting game of moving in to capitalize on so-called
policies which the West's most fervid enemy would be hard pressed to
devise in a more self-defeating pattern.

But with exuberant, politically-motivated assists from the stalwart,
macho defenders of American resources, honor, and integrity sent to
Washington to "serve the people," Israeli cuckolding is not limited to
eviscerating the grand designs of global policies. With that meticulous
attention to their own advantage in every detail which has facilitated the
efforts of Zionist leadership to sell their movement and its state as a "liberal,
emancipating, peace-loving" member of the world community, the same
leaders, governing Israel, find numerous delectable crumbs left over, here
and there, from the gluttonous feast which the stewards of American
taxpayers' funds put upon the Zionist table.

The "uncensored version" of the GAO report provides several
examples:

A little-advertised part of the Egyptian/Israeli treaty was an initial
commitment by the United States of $5 *billion* to help finance the redeploy-
ment of Israeli troops following the withdrawal from the Sinai and also to
assist the switchover of Egyptian dependency upon Soviet armaments to
American supplies. The figures were: $3.9 *billion* to Israel and $1.8 *billion*
to Egypt.[6] There have been continuing subsidies to both parties but these
details are not particularly relevant here.

Part of the grants to Israel were used for heavy construction machinery to build new bases, including two new military airfields (reputed to be
among the most modern in the world) to replace those abandoned in the
Sinai. The heavy equipment was "titled to Israel," in the GAO's language.
Because of the harsh conditions under which the equipment was used and
"around the clock" work, it was anticipated the equipment would be worn
out when the projects were completed. But "it did not break down as
anticipated" and Israel either sold "the items outside of Israel or transferred
them to other Israeli projects.

For example, approximately $1 million worth of structures, building
materials and office supplies was purchased by the multinational

peacekeeping organization in the Sinai. *Since the United States pays for the peacekeeping force along with Egypt and Israel this means it, in essence, repurchased part of the equipment.*[7] (Emphasis supplied)

In addition, $172 million of "construction equipment and building materials and supplies that remained were titled to the Government of Israel."[8] This practice is contrary to procedures followed in other countries. "Leaving construction equipment and excess materials and supplies behind is not the usual practice."[9]

Individual Americans emulating such financial skullduggery would soon find the Internal Revenue Service breathing down their necks and serving court orders to open their safety deposit boxes unless, as a few such notorious entrepreneurs have done, they escape to Costa Rica or Bimini first. But in support of the never-defined "special relationship" with our trusted and divinely ordained Middle East "ally" apparently there are not even any routine, computerized audits of accounts.

Claudia Wright wrote, with admirable candor, conclusions which almost any fair-minded reader of the GAO report would reach:

The report shows that Israeli officials *intentionally* mislead U.S. officials in private, just as they lie in public about these issues. They can usually do this without fear of private rebuke or public exposure because U.S. officials *allow the Israelis* to censor the record of bilateral negotiations and suppress the evidence of policy differences.[10] (Emphasis supplied)

The present book lifts many of the curtains hiding some of this record and assembles the facts in a pattern which should put more Americans on the alert. Hopefully, it will contribute sufficiently to public information to stimulate enough of them to call to account those American officials who have been—and are—derelict in their sworn responsibilities as stewards of American honor and treasure. For more than hard-to-come-by money is being offered on the altars of the voracious political appetites of national executives and legislators more interested in the perquisites of office than in national morality, more concerned with "the next election" than with persuading by example the hearts and minds of a bewildered world that what Abraham Lincoln called "the last best hope of earth" is, indeed worthy of the role.

The "loans" to the Zionist state still outstanding—if they are not all eventually forgiven—are made at rates which average less than 4 percent, and payment is stretched over extended periods of time. The combination of low interest and long repayment times (if the loans are ever repaid) must be the envy of those Americans frustrated by threatened mortgage foreclosures or faced with diminishing liquidity because of the restricted capital available to the Small Business Agency.

But this contrast between the generosity of United States subsidies to Israel and the bruising hardships produced by United States Government economic policies since January 1981, is not necessarily conclusive evidence of either the soundness or its lack in the American policy of aid to Israel. At times, the totality of the nation's global interests may outweigh discomfort for any segment of its population. This fact is accepted, for example, in time of war. All Americans ask is that, in such situations of hard choice, the sacrifices be warranted by the desired goal and be equitably shared. Foreign aid has been generally recognized as an instrument for advancing United States interests by advancing peace through the alleviation of hunger and disease, providing better communications, and building capital bases in the turbulent emergent nations of the world. The theory does not always work. Corruption, simple mismanagement, wrong ordering of any given nation's priorities have often defeated the generally good intentions. Too often, American aid is used to shore up local regimes which are repressive rather than liberating. Foreign aid then becomes self-defeating, at least in the estimation of those Americans who may still cling to the Jeffersonian dream and the Lincoln exhortation that it may be "the last best hope on earth."

If foreign aid has not produced the kind of world of which Americans dream, the disappointment may be mitigated by a guess as to how much worse what Haim Potok has called this "broken century" might have been without this help. Applying this relative yardstick to the Middle East, many Americans are seriously concerned about the size of aid to Israel because they cannot find sufficient evidence to prove the Zionist state has contributed much constructively to either closely defined United States interests or to the larger struggle for world peace. More than any other of the then-major powers, American political action from 1944 to 1948 was responsible for the United Nations recommendation to partition Palestine. The Zionist state was established as one consequence of this action and its survival became something of a matter of American honor. In the state's infant years, American aid was preponderantly economic. Table 1 of this study identifies $594.6 million of such assistance between 1949 and 1961. A mere $900,000—in the form of a loan—was the military aid for the same period. But the character of the U.S./Israeli relationship—and something of the transformation of the character of the Zionist state—is disclosed by the fact that since 1962, through fiscal year 1983, military aid has increased to more than $17 *billion,* nearly half in the form of grants. Economic aid, on the other hand, has increased from $86.5 million in the 1949–1952 period to just over $8 *billion* in the 1953–1983 years. To put it another way, in just over three decades, American military aid has increased something like seventeen fold, using the $1.7 *billion* for the current year as a yardstick. Economic aid over the same period has been multiplied about nine times over the 1949 figure, comparing the $86.5 million of that year with the $785 million Reagan requested in fiscal 1983.

Despite frequent boasts of Israel's officials about its ability to "go it alone," it appears even these massive American infusions failed to enable the state to take care of itself. On the contrary, they could well have conditioned the Zionist state to live beyond its means. From the viewpoint of the questioning American there seems to be no bottom to the barrel. Neither the military nor the economic aid has contributed to the stability and peace which American aid is intended to serve. United States aid has not stimulated greater economic opportunity for Israel's Arab minority. On the contrary it has helped perpetuate a kind of apartheid economy and social order in which Arabs are distinctly disadvantaged.[11] According to U.S. Public Law (94–329), the United States is prohibited from providing foreign aid to any country where "a consistent pattern of gross violations of international human rights"[12] exists. But the Department of State's most recent review of human rights practices in Israel glosses over the impact upon the Arab minority of Israel's Zionist legislation and of human rights violations in Israel. (Knowledge that the Arab minority is treated as second-class citizens certainly cannot contribute to Arab enthusiasm for peace.) But serious international consequences attach to extravagant American aid, so uncritically given. It has, for example, made it possible for Israel to fight its wars with "neither blood nor a bad taste in its mouth," to use the phrase Jacobo Timerman employs describing the June 1982 carpet bombing of Sidon and Tyre.[13] But superior war-making ability is not the only dividend the Zionist state collects from American aid. It can also—so far successfully —obstruct peace. A major part of American strategy has been to persuade Jordan's King Hussein (in some association with the Palestinians) to enter "the Camp David process." With unassailable logic, both the Jordanian monarch and Yassir Arafat, consulting with the king about the "association" recommended in Reagan's September 1, 1982 blueprint for peace, have so far declined. Both have said they find "positive elements" in the

Reagan proposals,[14] but both have indicated that a lack of confidence in American credibility has so far prevented them from any firm commitment to join substantive negotiations needed to make the Reagan proposals operative. After the first Arafat/Hussein meeting since 1970, Henry Tanner of the *New York Times,* on November 5, 1982 (pp. 1, 6), reported an interview with the king. The talks had been "inconclusive," Tanner observed, because the king admitted to Arafat he could offer no assurances of American response even if Arafat offered to "recognize Israel's right to exist."

The immediate test of American credibility for which the Arabs are asking, is that the United States insist Israel end its policy of increasing settlements in the West Bank. If there are any "quiet diplomacies" in which the United States is attempting to meet this test, the Israelis are still defiant. In fact, the Begin government greeted the September 1 declaration by announcing plans for three new settlements. Authoritative Zionist/Israeli statements have projected plans to increase the Zionist population of "Judea and Samaria" (the West Bank), to 100,000 by 1985. Realization of this goal, aided by American dollars, would virtually preclude any Israeli withdrawal and restoration of sovereignty to any Arab government, either Jordanian or Palestinian.

Washington's reaction has been reiteration of the banalities that such action is "not conducive to peace." The rhetoric is usually accompanied by assurances the United States does not intend to use foreign aid to Israel as a means of persuading the Zionist state to comply with either international law or the specific recommendations of the Reagan design for peace. So, the Israeli government/Zionist organization combine proceeds to allocate about $100 million annually for settlement expansion in "territory acquired by war."

A distinguished Israeli military man—General Mattatyahu Peled, former member of the General Staff—has offered one possible explanation for the bellicosity of the Zionist state and its policy of seeking "security" by acquiring more Arab territory rather than pursuing a political process of negotiating for a genuine peace. Peled observes that "more than 75 percent" of the latest (1983) package of $2.485 *billion* of American aid "can be expected to go to keeping up Israel's defense expenditure." As a result:

> One of the most dangerous consequences is that the standing army has come to play an independent role in the country's *political* decisions — in open violation of the clearly defined traditions that substitute, in Israel, for a written constitution. (emphasis supplied)

There are, he says, "no practical limits to Israeli defense spending."
The army can now:

> [F]ield a force larger than the one that fought in the Sinai without
> calling up the reserves—making it much easier for the Government to
> submit to the army's demands.

He quotes Rafael Eytan, Chief of Staff who, when asked why he advocated an invasion of Lebanon, answered:

> What do you suppose I have built a large modern army for?

This was in the summer of 1982, after "a year of unprecedented quiet on the Lebanese border." American aid, "careless in its giving," Peled continues, has produced a "military establishment . . . grown out of all proportion to our (Israel's) security needs." Finally, Peled asks "the American taxpayer,":

> Why are you giving us the rope with which to hang ourselves?[15]

A good question, indeed! Burdened American taxpayers, victims of the Reagan reductions in Federal support for social programs, apprehensive recipients of Social Security benefits, New York, Chicago and Cleveland refugees from heatless homes to warm community shelters and demoralized "firsters" on welfare all might ask their honorable Congressmen, Senators and the President of the United States when they will stop "sparing the rod and spoiling the child."

A judgment of American aid to Israel would be incomplete without one other explanation for its constant and steady expansion despite the often perceptible conflicts between Israeli policies and declared American interests. There are those in government and out who regard Israel as a "strategic asset." The President is among them. They deny that what many consider excessive American generosity is the result of what Peled calls "carelessness" or of the effectiveness of the Zionist lobby. "Israel," they say, "is America's only reliable ally in the Middle East." (They neglect to speculate that United States bias toward Israel is responsible for "Arab" lack of commitment to United States policies.) During the incumbency of Alexander Haig as Secretary of State this thinking evolved to the point where a formal agreement for "strategic cooperation" was under consideration. The negotiations were suspended by the United States when Israel "annexed" the Golan Heights.

But even without any such formal agreement it is an open secret that the military might of Israel has been used—and flaunted—to intimidate and occasionally to inflict actual defeat upon stirrings of native Arab nationalism. In 1956, Israel was an eager collaborator with the British and French in the tri-partite effort to thwart Nasser's control of the Suez Canal and, undoubtedly, to bring down the charismatic Egyptian himself. There is evidence of Israeli collaboration with the former Shah's efforts to keep the Kurdish pot boiling in Iraq in the hope of weakening the regime in Baghdad. There was collaboration between Israel and the hard core Colons in Algeria two decades ago. In 1970, Israel mobilized to threaten Syria, which was preparing to come to the defense of the Palestinians then under attack by Hussein in Jordan. Israel's support for the forces of Colonel Haddad in southern Lebanon nourished the Colonel's design to partition Lebanon and to establish an Israeli puppet-state in the south. Henry Kissinger once even threatened to unleash Israeli power against the oil producing Arabs of the Persian Gulf if the supply and pricing standards of those states did not conform to United States ideas of comfort.

Israel, of course, has had its own strategic objectives for all of these interventions in Arab affairs. An old Zionist political maxim was—and still is—"Arab disunity is Zionism's secret weapon." But many Arabs entertain more than a small suspicion that some of these unwelcome Zionist intrusions are also covert American designs. They are intended to frustrate progressive forces in the area, and the Zionist state is a willing—even an eager—proxy policeman. The Arab suspicions are circumstantially confirmed by the consistent failure of the United States to impose serious and effective sanctions upon Israel; and the more cynical observers in Washington and elsewhere also suspect the United States treats the Zionist state so gingerly because, in a crunch, the responsible authorities of the Middle East "ally" could spill some unsavory beans.

Supporters of this "strategic asset" vision of Israel regard United States aid as nothing more than payment for services rendered—or perhaps to be rendered at some future time. The swagger, the arrogance, the air of proprietorship which so often characterize the visit of a Zionist VIP to the United States lends some credence to this unadvertised partnership. Americans are simply advised "a special relationship" exists. But there is reluctance on the part of American officialdom to spell out the specifics.

The contributions of Israel to this school of American strategists are not limited to the Middle East and obstreperous Arabs intent on progressive regimes and genuine independence. American administrations—and Americans—who often appear to believe arms are a substitute for rational policies, regularly employ the Zionist state to huckster military equipment

to some of the most widely recognized, unsavory and anachronistic governments. Recently, another Israeli, uncomfortable with this "merchants of
death" role for his country, contributed a tongue-in-cheek disclosure.
American "liberals" who either have not known this or who, if they have
known it, have chosen not to talk about it for fear of tarnishing the
orchestrated virtues of the Zionist state should read it and weep—and
reassess their mesalliance. Benjamin Beit-Hallahmi teaches psychology at
Israel's Haifa University. "Israelis now see their country as an equal partner
of the United States in a number of troubled third-world countries,"[16] he
writes. But the partnership is not "to loose the fetters of wickedness, to
undo the bands of the yoke and to let the oppressed go free."[17] Rather:

> Throughout the third world, Israel has succeeded where other Western
> powers have failed in using force to blunt the edge of native radicalism.
> And they do it with what Washington sees as aplomb, enthusiasm and
> grace. The Reagan Administration cannot send military advisors to
> Zaire, Guatemala, South Africa or Haiti. Nor would many of Ameri-
> ca's European allies willingly aid repressive regimes like, say, the
> Chilean Junta.

That is about as representative a list of rogue-gallery governments as it
is possible to assemble. Reinforcing them, Beit-Hallahmi says, many would
regard as "dirty work." But Israelis consider it:

> [A] defensible duty and even, in some cases, an exalted calling.

Israeli governments are able to engage in these edifying enterprises
because:

> There is virtually no Israeli opposition to this global adventurism.
> There is no "human rights lobby" to oppose military involvement in
> Guatemala, Haiti or South Africa. There are no angry editorials or
> demonstrations when officials from repressive third-world countries
> visit Jerusalem. The signing in March of a cultural cooperation and
> exchange treaty with Haiti—which in most countries would have
> created a wave of protest or at least a wave of sad jokes—aroused no
> interest whatsoever in Israel. When Israeli military advisors train
> Angola Unita forces in Namibia, there are no angry Congressional
> reactions and no oversight committees. . . . Indeed, many Israelis feel
> their support for *United States interests* around the world should earn
> them special consideration from Washington and the American
> public . . .
>   The role of regional and global policeman is something that many

Israelis find attractive, and they are ready to go on with the job—for which they expect to be handsomely rewarded. (emphasis supplied)

To which many Americans would say, "How fulsome is handsome?"

Making Israel the American surrogate for snuffing out progressive forces in the Middle East coincides with the regional strategies of the Zionist state. Making the Zionist state the door-to-door peddler of the Pentagon's closeouts to some of the most unsavory regimes of the world synchronizes with an Israeli economy, 40% of which is committed to the production of military hardware. Never mind that such an imbalance in its productivity contributes heavily to Israel's 135% inflation-rate. Never mind that the state "the Jewish people" needed to "end its homelessness" is now faced with an emigration exceeding the numbers of "exiles" seeking to be "ingathered."[18] These are Israel's problems. In a way, they may fulfill "the promise" Menahem Begin employs so glibly to justify Israel's expansionism. Only this fulfillment comes in a way the erstwhile terrorist does not intend. It completes "the promise" by supplying a part Begin elects never to mention. But Jeremiah, one of the authentic interpreters of "the promise" was not so reticent:

Among My people are found wicked men;
They pry, as fowlers lie in wait;
They set a trap, they catch men.
As a cage is full of birds,
So are their homes full of deceit;
Therefore, they are become great, and waxen rich;
They are waxen fat, they are become sleek;
Yea, they exceed in deeds of wickedness;
They plead not the cause of the fatherless
And the right of the needy do they not judge.
Shall I not punish for these things?
Saith the Lord;
Shall not My soul be avenged
On such a nation as this? (5:26–29)

These questions are not for the Zionist state alone to answer. American aid is complicitous in these transgressions, thwarting liberation, substituting swords for ploughshares. American Jews who give "charity" uncritically are culpable. They have a public responsibility to know what it is they support, the displacement of another people, the underpinning for a discriminatory social and economic system. The Zionist state is perceived in many places as an insignia of the United States. Before another dollar is given, *all* Americans should ask *themselves* if the kind of interests Israel supports for us represents the kind of America we wish to have and have the world recognize. It is all very well to assure Israel of our guarantees for its security. But in return, the United States has the right—even the obligation to its own integrity and to world peace—to demand that the Zionist state end its addiction to domestic policies of discrimination and its reliance upon "made-in-America" swords in its futile, thirty year war against its neighbors and its attempted genocide of the Palestinians as the road to "recognition" and "security." In his book of passionate disillusion, Jacobo Timerman agonizes that Israel has:

> [R]eturned to the ghetto, to the mood that prevailed in the ghetto. . . . Why is it that we have locked ourselves into a ghetto once again, waiting for the rich uncle from America to help us endure?[19]

In another place Timerman rejects the euphoric Israeli and American predictions at the beginning of the war in Lebanon that the Israeli invasion offered "Jerusalem and Washington . . . an array of opportunities." He finds the Palestinians "were preparing to recognize Israel before we invaded Lebanon and even now, despite their present difficulties, they have signalled enough political openings, which should be seized by the Israeli government." War, he contends, offers no opportunities. "Peace is the only opportunity."[20]

But there is scant hope for the Shamir government to come to this conclusion in the near future. And an American administration that has consistently substituted armaments for diplomacy is unlikely to press Israel to do so. The present book's final chapter, "Shamir: Government of Continuity," ends with this question, ". . . what should the United States expect in return for its assistance?" Shamir gave the answer at the November talks when he rejected out of hand the Reagan appeal for modification of the Lebanon-withdrawal agreement and the freezing of settlements. Why should an Israeli government alter its policies to accommodate the United States when the United States rewards Israel for refusing to do so? If this is a way to successful negotiations for American interests, what is left of the meaning of the old maxim that it is always better to negotiate from strength? The "new" agreement for U.S./Israeli military and political cooperation suggests that United States peace-seeking energies, weak and indecisive as they have been, will now be harnessed to Israeli dynamics for expansion, hegemony and violations of human rights.

In a particularly striking editorial (December 2, 1983, p. 28) *The Wall Street Journal* says:

> One Israeli participant in the recently concluded U.S.-Israeli strategic talks remarked that in all his years of meetings with the U.S. government, this was the first time that not a single State Department official had murmured a word about how America needed to cooperate with the PLO.

This Israeli version may be another example of Ms. Wright's charge "that many Israeli claims . . . are bald-faced lies."[21] But assuming its accuracy, it is consistent with the Reagan Administration's denigration of the PLO and its resistance to any genuine Palestinian self-determination. In this sense, American policy has retrogressed from even the Carter government's reluctant acceptance of the centrality of the problem of the Palestinians to any proposals for a viable peace. The beneficences handed the Zionist state at these November meetings are consistent with the formula of Secretary of State, Mr. Shultz, to "spare the rod and spoil the child" because then the obstreperous, macho-loving dependent will eventually mature into an agreeable, cooperative, peace-loving adult.

But nothing in Shamir's career supports such naivete. The present Prime Minister lacks most of Begin's flambuoyancy and (for some) charisma. Washington will, nevertheless, do well to heed a characterization by one of Israel's own, most prominent political commentators:

> Assessing Mr. Shamir's reputation as a formidable fighter . . . Philip Gillon borrowed a quotation from Lord Byron: "The mildest manner'd man that ever scuttled ship or cut a throat."

Reverting to *The Wall Street Journal*'s editorial, the State Department is not the White House and the PLO may, or may not surmount its difficulties to remain the "sole, legitimate representative of the Palestinian people."[22] But the Palestinians will remain. The seeds of the escalating and increasingly threatening Middle East conflict are generally identified as Zionist/Israeli unremitting denials of the political and human rights of the indigenous Palestinians. All peace formulas have failed because the "great powers" have refused to compel the Zionist state to comply with international law and world political consensus calling for rectification of the Israeli violations of these Palestinian rights. Consequently, there has never been any Zionist atonement or indemnification for what Uri Davis, a genuinely emancipated Israeli scholar, has called "the original sin." If, indeed, the Washington "fixers" are more interested in a real peace than in a thinly-disguised employment of American power laundered through Israel to dominate the majority peoples of the area, they would be well-advised to heed the old Santayana warning that "those who cannot remember the past are condemned to repeat it"; or, the old Frenchman, Talleyrand's exquisitely cynical description of a great statesman as one who "anticipates the inevitable." Not a penny of America's billions has gone to fundamentally righting the political wrongs and the human indignities suffered by the Palestinians at the hands of exclusivist Zionism. On the contrary—and perversely—all the American largesse has simply reinforced the determination of Israel's Zionist rulers, with Shamir as a legitimate, unreconstructed, lineal descendant, to pursue the single-minded policies reflected in such exalting comments as Golda Meir's "the Palestinians do not exist" or her reflection that "every night when I go to bed I worry about how many Arab babies will be born." That spirit, flaunted by Begin, implied clearly in Shamir's gutteral English, remains dominant in the "Government of Continuity." Not until further American aid is strictly conditioned by the unambiguous demand that the Zionist recipients pursue diplomacy and peace rather than expansion and war can such profligate dispensing of American resources be justified either morally or politically.

Peace is not to be found at the end of an M-14 in the hands of an Israeli or in the bomb-sights of an F-15 zeroing in on some new Arab city. Peace is to be found now—as for the six decades of Zionist colonizing and aggression—in recognizing the humanity of the Palestinians, their national identity, and their right to a flag and a passport of their own. To assist the Israelis to recognize this central fact, to insist upon such recognition as the only acceptable Israeli concession for further American aid is the moral—as well as the necessary political—responsibility of Americans.

Elmer Berger
Longboat Key, Florida
March 1, 1984

INTRODUCTION

The establishment of Israel in 1948 was a product of a long-term campaign by the World Zionist Organization (WZO) to establish a "Jewish homeland" in Palestine—a campaign that began long before the ascendance of Adolf Hitler to power in Germany and that was long supported by Britain and the U.S. In 1914, when World War I broke out, Chaim Weizmann, President of the WZO, saw an opportunity to promote his political program for Palestine by siding with the Western democracies.[1] Britain, which was desperately searching for allies to turn the tide of war, was willing to espouse Zionism. It did so because it needed the support of the European Jewry behind its war effort as well as loans for the war chest from American financial institutions, where there was much Jewish influence. In November 1917, Arthur James Balfour, Britain's Foreign Minister, issued his famous Declaration, expressing his government's intent to "favor the establishment in Palestine of a national home for the Jewish people" and promising to "use their best endeavours to facilitate the achievement of this object."[2]

Unfortunately, the Balfour Declaration was issued at the same time that the British had promised the Arabs to support their independence from Ottoman rule, if they fought, which they did, with the Allies against Germany and the Ottomans.[3] These irreconcilable pledges were made out of desperation when Britain had its back against the wall. There would be time to worry about them after the war, when a compromise could be fashioned. As it turned out, Britain managed to avoid the dilemma of choosing between Arabs and Jews by asking the League of Nations to put Palestine under a British mandate.

In response to Zionist pressure to make good on its promises, Britain allowed, regardless of the wishes of the Palestinian people, Jewish immigration into Palestine in the 1920s and 1930s. Such a stop-gap measure provided Zionism with an opportunity to establish a toehold in the Arab World. London had the backing of the U.S., which had endorsed the Balfour Declaration in the final days of the war. Some American and British officials hoped that "a Jewish majority might develop in Palestine in the course of time, and that a Jewish state might thus be the ultimate outcome of the Balfour Declaration."[4]

Britain secured the approval of the Kingdom of Hijaz for Jewish immigration into Palestine only after it had acknowledged and guaranteed independence for the Arabs. The steady flow of immigrants resulted in a sharp increase in the Jewish population, swelling from 50,000 at the close of the war to 445,000 in 1939, not quite one-third of the total population.[5] As early as 1917 and throughout the 1920s, the Palestinian Arabs protested against and acted to halt the increase in Jewish immigration and, in 1936, called a general strike. The Arab-Jewish hostility led to Britain's issuance of a White Paper in May 1939, limiting Jewish immigration[6] in an effort to placate the Arabs.

The White Paper marked the beginning of an intensified campaign by Zionism to get the U.S. to act on their behalf to reverse its terms.[7] With the outbreak of World War II, Zionist leaders moved the center of their activities to the U.S. in order to rally American Jewish and non-Jewish support behind their program. They conducted intensive campaigns to influence the American public and to solicit their support for removing British restrictions on Jewish immigration and for eventual establishment of a Zionist state in Palestine.[8] They exploited the conditions of the displaced Jews in Europe to propagate the idea that Palestine was the only solution for the Jewish problem. At the height of the refugee problem in the middle of the war, Zionist leaders bitterly attacked proposals put forward by President Franklin D. Roosevelt to find a permanent solution for displaced Jews on a world-wide basis. They flatly rejected his proposal to open the doors of many nations to Jewish refugees after the war.[9] Zionists did not want to disperse Jewish refugees in many countries but, instead, to promote their program for Palestine.

Although Roosevelt resisted Zionist pressure and sought to avoid alienating the Arabs—whose support was vital to the Allied war effort in North Africa and the Middle East—his successor, Harry S Truman, was more sympathetic to Zionism and had already gone on record when he was a Senator supporting the creation of a Jewish homeland in Palestine.[10] He therefore was receptive to Zionist pressure and put his Democratic Party's interest in both mid-term and national elections above the rights of the Arab Palestinians. In doing so, he failed to heed the advice of the State and Defense Departments to refrain from making Palestine a major campaign issue during his years in office.[11] Instead, his actions brought the Palestine issue directly into the arena of U.S. domestic politics.

Realizing his likely political advantage in espousing the Zionist cause, Truman broke away from the joint American-British diplomatic efforts to find a solution acceptable to both Arabs and Zionists. Instead, he acted on his own, motivated primarily by an interest in strengthening his chances for obtaining the presidential nomination of his party in 1948 and his electoral victory in the November election.[12] Consequently, he gave his blessing in May 1948 to the Zionist-planned announcement for the establishment of Israel and wasted no time in granting it U.S. recognition.[13] His political ambition blurred his vision entirely to the Zionist use of terrorism in forcibly evicting the Christian and Muslim populations from Palestine as part of the effort to make room for European Zionists to found their state in the midst of the Arab world.

Truman and his successors have consistently tilted in favor of Israel and have provided it with massive military and economic assistance to ensure its security and economic well-being. Democratic and Republican politicians alike have advocated more support and more aid for Israel in order to demonstrate that they are the proven friends of the prosperous and influential American Jewish community. In the scramble for Jewish financial and political backing, presidential candidates of both parties have used Israel as a means to attract the so-called Jewish votes in such large metropolitan areas as New York, Chicago, Philadelphia, Miami, and Los Angeles. The electoral system for presidential election makes the ethnic balloting in these urban areas a significant factor in determining the success or failure of a presidential candidate. Political candidates have courted Jewish businessmen and Jewish organizations to obtain contributions for their campaigns to meet the ever increasing campaign costs of primaries and elections. They often appear to outbid each other in making pro-Israel statements in order to gain the financial and political backing of the Jewish community.[14] As a result, they have become susceptible to Jewish lobbying arguments that more assistance to Israel is needed in order to develop its economy and to help defend itself against its Arab neighbors. Thus, American politicians have allowed the Jewish minority—about three percent of the total population—to influence U.S. policy toward the Middle East to an extent far beyond its numerical representation in America.

American policy toward Israel has been shaped in part by a sense of guilt over the U.S. failure to help the persecuted Jews to escape Hitler's concentration camps and gas chambers. In fact, the U.S. immigration laws restricted the number of Jews, among others, who could immigrate before and during World War II. American Jews suffer from the same guilt feelings for the inadequacy of their assistance to the European Jews during the holocaust. This prompts many of them, even those who oppose Zionism as a philosophy, to contribute generously to Israel, to live in Israel for some time, or to join Jewish organizations to promote the welfare of the Zionist state. Guilt has also played a large role in persuading non-Zionist American Jews and Christian liberals to support Israel. Israel is viewed by many American politicians as "poor little Israel" or as the helpless "Hebrew David" against the massive "Arab Goliath." Such caricatures have distorted the complex issues underlying the Palestine Question, the single most important issue influencing U.S.-Arab relations, which threatens, in the long run, U.S. interests in the Middle East.

The U.S. media, which plays an important role in shaping American public opinion, is largely responsible for distorting the historical record in its coverage of the Arab-Israeli conflict. It has misinformed the public on the Palestine problem and has given little attention to the subhuman living conditions of the Arab refugees who were forcibly driven out of their homes in order to make Palestine a haven for the Zionists. The media have also distorted the Palestinian struggle, misrepresenting its aims and ignoring its programs, which are designed to restore the inalienable rights of the Palestinian people, including their right to self-determination and to the establishment of their own independent state.

Over the years, a barrage of pro-Israeli and anti-Arab propaganda has filled the media, stressing Judaeo-Christian heritage and the cultural affinity between Israel and the West in an attempt to influence American public opinion to give total support to Israel against the Eastern Arab Muslims, who are culturally and racially different. Thus, subtle ethnic animosities and biases have been injected into the Arab-Israeli conflict to swing public opinion in favor of Israel, which was generally presented as the underdog until the late 1960s.

The establishment of Israel in 1948 marked the beginning of a unique relationship between Israel and the U.S. Both Democratic and Republican Presidents have made "Israel's security and economic well-being . . . a basic and unshakable tenet of American foreign policy in the Middle East,"[15] even at times when the two governments have been at odds with each other; as, for example, over the treatment of Palestinians, the Zionist settlements in the territories occupied by Israel since 1967, the use of U.S.-made weapons in non-defensive wars, and Israeli actions reflecting an aggressive, expansionist policy in the region. Over the decades, both Democratic and Republican administrations have provided Israel with substantial military and economic assistance in order to enable Israel "to maintain its qualitative and technological superiority over any potential combination of regional (Arab) forces."[16] Its lion's share in the U.S. foreign aid program has made Israel, a tiny Zionist state with slightly more than three million population, the largest single recipient of American foreign assistance.

The amount and the impact of this American support to Israel is unmeasured and unmatched, despite the fact that there is no formal alliance that binds the U.S. with Israel. At most, there exists a generally stated U.S. commitment for the security of Israel.[17] Hence, the U.S. has often made Israel's objectives and needs the basis for its actions and policies in the region, regardless of other legal, moral and humanitarian considerations and regardless of objectives stemming from the U.S.'s vast economic and strategic interests in the Arab world.

In recent years, the U.S. assistance has caused some contention between the two governments because of continuing Israeli use of American-made weapons in offensive wars, which is in violation of U.S. law. Thus, following the invasion of southern Lebanon in 1978, Israel installed U.S.-made armored equipment there and refused repeated American requests for its removal. Even when the Israelis claimed that they had removed the equipment, U.S. satellites showed otherwise. President Jimmy Carter was outraged by Israel's false claims and threatened to ask Congress to halt arms sales to Israel unless these weapons were removed from southern Lebanon. It was only then that the Israeli government bowed to his pressure.[18]

The same controversy surfaced again during the Israeli military invasion of Lebanon in the summer of 1982. Israel's widespread use of U.S.-made cluster bombs against Lebanese and Palestinian civilians in violation of U.S. law led President Ronald Reagan to suspend the shipment of such weapons to Israel. U.S.-Israeli relations have been further strained as a result of the slaughter of hundreds of Palestinian refugees at the Sabra and Shatila camps in West Beirut in September, 1982, and Israel's refusal to withdraw from Lebanon.

The Reagan administration has faulted Israel for the massacres because Morris Draper, the Deputy Assistant Secretary of State for the Middle East, had "warned Israeli officials on the eve of the massacres against allowing the Phalangists into the camps."[19] It was also reported that the Israeli army guarding the camps allowed the Phalangist militiamen to enter the grounds at a time when the Israeli Defense Minister Ariel Sharon suspected that the Phalangists would murder the Palestinian civilians.[20] The massacres have raised a dilemma for the U.S., which had guaranteed the safety of the Palestinians after the withdrawal of the Palestine Liberation Organization (PLO) from West Beirut.[21] It has led some Americans to raise questions about U.S. governmental aid to Israel. Such criticism stems from the reports that American assistance funds are used to finance the erection of Israeli settlements in the occupied West Bank.[22] This revelation is embarrassing to the Republican administration, which has opposed the building of settlements in the occupied Arab land and has called for a freeze on new ones. Furthermore, Israel has flatly rejected the Reagan initiative seeking to find a peaceful solution for the Arab-Israeli conflict and has defiantly announced plans to construct new settlements in the West Bank.[23]

Due to the controversies surrounding the settlement issue and the Israeli use of U.S.-made weapons in non-defensive wars, it is timely to examine the nature and scope of American aid to Israel from its inception in 1948. Such an examination will shed light on the impact of U.S. military and economic assistance on Israel's ability "... to maintain its technological edge and its qualitative military advantage"[24] in the Middle East and to uphold and develop its ailing economy. Arab critics believe that unlimited U.S. support has created a monster out of Israel, able to act at will to implement its expansionist policy in the Middle Eastern region. Other observers argue that U.S. aid has led Israel to harden its position on the Palestinian Question and on the settlement for the long-standing Arab-Israeli conflict; they note that, so far, U.S. administrations have refused to use the leverage of massive U.S. military and economic assistance to persuade Israel to trade territories for peace in the Middle East.[25] Also, Israeli officials have often gained the help of the "American Jewish community" and organizations in dealing with U.S. administrations, especially during mid-term and presidential elections, to secure more aid and to extract promises not to pressure Israel to reach a broader settlement for the Arab-Israeli conflict. This is because the Israeli government has no intention of returning the occupied land to the Arab neighbors; instead, the Likud government has an imperial design for territorial expansion to form Greater Israel that will encompass large tracts of Arab land.

In order to shed light on the extent of U.S. assistance to Israel, this study is divided into three parts. The first will analyze the role played by the U.S. in helping Israel build a formidable military force and, over the decades, to maintain a military balance favoring Israel in the region. It will also examine U.S. economic assistance, which although it has taken many forms, has consistently served to help Israel meet the high cost of its military buildup and the challenges of economic development. The second part will scrutinize the substance and direction of Israel's policies in order to shed light on what appears to be in store for the rest of this decade, particularly the prospects for peace in the Middle East and its implications for the U.S. The last part contains an unabridged text of the report on U.S.

assistance to Israel prepared by the U.S. General Accounting Office (GAO), including information deleted from the final report released to the public in June 1983. It is a timely and important study since it offers an official account of the scale of American aid to Israel since 1948 as well as Israel's ability to pay a foreign debt of $21.5 billion, the highest per capita in the world.

Part One

1

U.S. MILITARY ASSISTANCE: AN ANALYSIS

The U.S., having helped establish Israel in the midst of the Arab world, has become its major political and financial backer. For domestic political and strategic considerations, the U.S. has felt obliged to assist Israel in safeguarding its independence, upholding its economy, and overcoming the financial burden of building up a superior military force in the Middle Eastern region. This was evident from the outset when Truman decided—within a few days of the creation of Israel—to approve an emergency loan of $100 million to help the Zionist leaders put their house in order and finance their industrial development projects.[26] From that time on, all U.S. administrations—Democratic and Republican alike— have been responsive to Israel's needs and pleas for more aid to provide substance to American assurances that the U.S. would be a dependable friend. Consequently, Israel has consistently been treated as a "special case" in the allocation of foreign economic and military assistance.

From 1949–1984, the U.S. government has given Israel a total of $28.1 billion (42.3 billion in 1983 U.S. dollars); military assistance has totaled $19.1 billion (28.8 billion in 1983 U.S. dollars), while economic aid has amounted to $8.95 billion (13.6 billion in 1983 U.S. dollars). In addition, the Export-Import Bank has extended $1.1 billion (1.6 billion in 1983 U.S. dollars) in loans to Israel between 1949–1983. In fact, U.S. governmental assistance has grown in volume, increasing from a small fraction of Israel's foreign transfers and loans in the early 1960s to over 80 percent of such transactions by 1979.[27] Thus, U.S. aid has become "an integral part of Israel's annual budget planning."[28]

It should be noted that U.S. aid has been instrumental in helping Israel to deal with its ailing economy and to meet its ever increasing military expenditures. Even U.S. economic assistance has had both economic and military implications in Israel. First, it has contributed to the development of Israel's industrial base, including its arms industry, which has been used for export to generate needed hard currency and capital to finance Israel's huge military expenditure. Second, U.S. aid has relieved the pressure on Israel's domestic revenue sources that otherwise would have been diverted to fund the armament program. A recent study reveals that "the vast majority, if not all U.S. economic assistance, is treated as a fungible resource by Israel." It also stated that "there is some discrepancy in the way Israel allocates resources generated internally compared to fungible resources received from the U.S."[29]

U.S. governmental assistance is a crucial mainstay of Israel's continuing ability to finance development projects and military expenditures. If it were not for substantial U.S. loans and grants, Israel would not have been able to tackle the serious economic problems it has been facing since its founding in 1948. Even Israeli records provide some evidence for this view. First, there is the long-standing pattern of Israeli deficits in its trade with other countries. While there has been a modest growth in the Israeli Gross National Product (GNP) over the years, Israel has steadily increased its military expenditures since 1948, both in dollar amount and as a proportion of expenditures: allocations for defense have risen from 30 percent of its GNP in 1975 to 40 percent in 1982. In view of these facts, it would have been difficult for Israel to meet its increasing military expenditures throughout the last three and a half decades without U.S. aid to fill the void. Nor could Israel have been in a position to finance the wars it has been waging in the area since 1948. Israel would not have been able to maintain its qualitative and technological edge over the neighboring Arab states.

The above mentioned arguments have been significantly substantiated by the publication of the report by The General Accounting Office on U.S. Aid to the State of Israel. The inclusion of this uncensored, though incomplete, version of the report will provide a clear understanding of the official American justification and arguments for its unconditional support of Israel.

Military Assistance: The Facts

Table 1 shows that the U.S. has given more military than economic assistance to Israel since 1949; military assistance amounted to $19.1 billion, or 68 percent of the total U.S. governmental assistance. These billions of dollars have been given to Israel to fulfill the historical commitment the U.S. made at the time that Israel was created. Truman and his successors guaranteed the survival and security of Israel with complete disregard for the rights of the Arab Palestinians who were forcibly evicted from Palestine so that the Zionist Europeans could establish "a Jewish homeland." American policy-makers realized that Israel can continue to exist only by force in the face of the challenges posed first by the Arab states and later by the eruption of Palestinian armed struggle under the PLO leadership.

TABLE 1

U.S. Governmental Assistance, 1949-1985

(Millions of Dollars)

	Military Assistance			Economic Assistance			
	Loans	*Grants*	*Sub-Total*	*Loans*	*Grants*	*Sub-Total*	*Total*
1949–1952	—	—	—	—	86.5	86.5	86.5
1953–1961	0.9	—	0.9	248.3	258.9	507.2	508.1
1962–1976	3,461.6	2,450	5,911.6	931.3	1,048	1,979.3	7,890.9
1977–1983	6,900.0	4,600	11,500	1,044.9	4,420	5,464.9	16,964.9
1984	850.0	850	1,700	—	910	910.0	2610.0
Total	11,212.5	7,900	19,112.5	2,224.5	6,793.4	8,947.9	28,060.4

Sources: U.S., Agency for International Development, Bureau for Program Policy and Coordination, *U.S. Overseas Loans and Grants and Assistance from International Organizations: Obligations and Loan Authorizations, July 1, 1945–June 30, 1971; July 1, 1945–September 30, 1977; July 1, 1945–September 30, 1979; and July 1, 1945–September 30, 1981. The New York Times*, August 10, 1982; *The Washington Post*, December 18, 1982. *The Mideast Observer in Washington*, April 15, 1983.

To support Israel's security, U.S. administrations have provided it with massive military assistance intended to strengthen its military capabilities and to enable it "to maintain (its) security against threats from the outside and from radical forces within the region."[30] In exchange, the U.S. has relied on Israel to divert the energies of some Arab states from development to confrontation with the aim of fostering their economic and political dependency. Others, mainly Zionists, argue that the purpose of American aid to Israel is to promote and defend Western values and interests in the highly strategic Middle Eastern region in the face of mounting threats by the Soviet Union. As a result, the U.S. has bankrolled Israel's arms purchases and has transferred to Israel advanced conventional weapons, other military equipment, and services in an effort to make Israel a military force superior to any force that could be assembled by any combination of the Arab states.[31] Notably, as much as $7.9 billion out of the $19.1 billion in military assistance have been given to Israel as outright grants. The U.S. also has become Israel's major arms supplier, providing it with the most sophisticated weaponry in the American arsenal to beef up its military capability far beyond security requirements. For example, by 1975, the U.S. supplied Israel with F-15 Eagle fighters which could outperform the MIG-23 that Egypt and Syria had acquired from the Soviet Union. Israel also received the Lance surface-to-surface guided missiles which could deliver both conventional and nuclear warheads over a 70-mile range. Such a missile system is "five times more effective than the Soviet-made Scud B missiles in Syria and Egypt."[32] There is a danger that these missiles can be used to deliver nuclear warheads since it is believed that Israel has "at least ten nuclear bombs with a 20-kiloton yield—the size of the U.S. atom bomb dropped on Nagasaki."[33]

U.S. actions have contributed to the escalation of the arms race in the Middle East, since the Arab frontline states have sought to match Israeli armaments in order to fill the military void. Furthermore, U.S. military assistance has given Israel formidable military power that has been used to carry out territorial expansion; the Arab states have been at a military disadvantage and Israel has been able to pursue its expansionary actions without fear of Arab retaliation because the U.S., until recently, has refused to sell advanced weapons to Israel's immediate neighbors.

The U.S. role is evident in the flexibility Israel has been granted in disposing of U.S. military assistance. First, Israel is one of two nations that have been permitted to order U.S. equipment through the security assistance program, that is, prior to congressional approval of the appropriations. Second, it is one of five countries that have been allowed to spend U.S. military assistance funds in countries other than the U.S. Third, it has been given unprecedented privileges to bid for U.S. defense contracts. Fourth, it has been allowed to acquire the most sophisticated U.S. weaponry and military electronics. Fifth, the Israeli arms industry has been permitted to obtain strategic U.S. technology and equipment to build up its advanced weapon production. For example, Pratt and Whitney, the engine manufacturing subsidiary of the giant United Technologies Corporation, is helping Israel develop an engine for an advanced supersonic-speed fighter aircraft—the Lavi—that will be completed in the 1980s.[34]

Israel has not only been given grants totalling $7.9 billion between 1974–1984 but also is one of the few countries identified as a potential recipient of low-interest loans. In addition, it has been permitted 30-year repayment with a grace period on the repayment of principal for the first ten years of the loan.[35] In fact, the huge annual U.S. military assistance has taken care of paying back the loans as well as acquiring new weaponry from the U.S.

Israel has provided the U.S. with an opportunity to test American weapons in the battlefield and to recommend changes to improve their performance. Israel has always used these recommendations as a means to obtain more advanced American weapons in return for such service. Israel and the U.S. have also shared intelligence information. In that swap, Israel has received intelligence reports obtained by U.S. satellites. Israel has also sold the U.S. large quantities of Israeli-made weapons in an effort to help Israel deal with a worsening balance-of-payments deficit. In 1975, for example, Israel's deficit was running at $3 billion. Notably, American purchases are helpful to Israel's foreign exchange problems because of American support of Israel's arms industry, which is the largest foreign exchange earner among Israeli products.

1962: The Turning Point

Table 1 reveals that 1962 was a turning point in the U.S. aid program, marking a major shift in the allocations of aid between military and economic assistance. Prior to 1962, Israel received very little military assistance. Between 1949 and 1961, for example, total U.S. military assistance amounted to less than one million dollars, while economic assistance totaled $594.6 million. In addition, the Export-Import Bank supplied Israel with $192 million in loans during this period. The Truman and Eisenhower administrations, seeing no direct military threats to Israel in the aftermath of the defeat of the Arab armies in 1948, concentrated on economic assistance to help Israel develop its economy and maintain political stability. The small size of military assistance was prompted by both military and political considerations. Militarily, Israel did not need U.S.-made weapons at this time since its weapons were European and it needed spare parts and additional arms from Europe to augment its arsenal. In fact, Britain and France were Israel's major arms suppliers during the 1950s. Politically, the Truman administration temporarily shifted its focus away from the Middle East to other geographical regions where communist threats were much greater. Between 1949–1952, Truman was preoccupied by (1) European reconstruction and rehabilitation under the Marshall Plan after the devastating effect that World War II had on European economies; (2) U.S. concern about the cold war, which culminated in the formation of the North Atlantic Treaty Organization (NATO) and its efforts to build up Western defenses to contain communist threats in Europe; and (3) the outbreak of the Korean War, which was financed by the U.S. and fought under the U.N. banner.

The election of President Dwight Eisenhower in 1952 marked a new drive by the U.S. to form regional military alliances to contain communism in the most strategically important regions of the world, including the Middle East.[36] Secretary of State John Foster Dulles sought to improve relations with the Arab states, especially Egypt, because of the Suez Canal,[37] and to persuade them to join the Western-promoted Middle East defense organization. He did not want to antagonize the Arab governments by giving military assistance to Israel as long as there was a chance that a regional alliance could be formed to stop Soviet penetration into the Middle East. When Iraq became a founder of the Baghdad Pact in 1954, American officials courted Egyptian and other Arab governments in the hope that they could join the U.S.-sponsored pact to combat communism in the region.

In 1962, the initiation of the Foreign Assistance Act, under President John F. Kennedy, ushered in a new era in the U.S. foreign aid program. It was born at a time when the relations between Washington and Moscow were strained and the international atmosphere was charged with cold-war competition. Both super powers were using foreign aid as a means to further their own national interests in the Middle East and elsewhere. The Kennedy administration persuaded Congress to approve foreign-aid legislation, which committed the U.S. to furnish military assistance to friendly nations for "the common defense against internal and external aggression."

This was primarily because U.S. efforts "to promote peace and security continue to require measures of support based upon the principles of effective self-help and mutual aid."[38]

This legislation reversed the trend that existed previously under the Republican administration. It resulted in an astronomical rise in the volume of U.S. aid to Israel and in a major shift in the allocation of this aid between economic and military assistance—changes that continued under Kennedy's Democratic and Republican successors. The U.S. provided Israel with substantial economic assistance, increasing from $594.6 million between 1949-1961 to $2 billion between 1962-1976. The increase in U.S. military assistance was phenomenal, rising from less than one million dollars between 1949-1961 to as much as $5.9 billion between 1962-1976. As a result, military assistance to Israel accounted for 75 percent of total U.S. governmental assistance during this recent period.

This substantial increase in U.S. military assistance was a reaction to Soviet gains in influence in the Middle East and to a sharp decline that had taken place in Western influence during a time of rising Arab nationalism. With the cold-war fever running high in Washington, the Kennedy administration thought that Israel could be used to counter Soviet influence in the Middle East. American policy-makers advocated massive military assistance to Israel, then, as a way to block Soviet designs on the region and to offset the newly acquired Soviet-made armaments by Egypt and Syria.

Israeli officials, taking advantage of U.S. apprehension about Soviet moves in the Middle East, appealed to Washington for more and better arms to defend itself against the Soviet-backed Arab states. The U.S. responded generously to Israeli requests by embarking on an ambitious and costly program to help Israel complete renovation of its armed forces, which until then had been European-equipped.

Kennedy and his successors poured $6 billion into Israel to modernize its armed forces between 1962-1976. Sophisticated American weapons were sold to Israel as a way to establish and maintain its military superiority over its Arab neighbors. In doing so, the U.S. made a long-term commitment to furnish Israel with the most advanced American weaponry; this commitment reflected a deliberate plan by the U.S. to tilt the military balance permanently in favor of Israel, thus placing the Arab states at a disadvantage. The U.S. denied Arab states access to such advanced weapons.

The 1967 War: Johnson Rewards Israeli Aggression

The untimely death of Kennedy did not affect the flow of U.S. aid to Israel. Although President Lyndon B. Johnson primarily concentrated on the Vietnam conflict, he did not forget Israel. His deep distrust for the wars of national liberation affected his attitude toward the Palestine problem. His preoccupation with a military victory for the Vietnam conflict led him to increase aid to Israel to promote American strategic and economic interests in the Middle East as well as to counter the growing Soviet influence there. American officials saw Soviet influence in Egypt as a threat to the southern flank of the NATO, to the naval and communications lanes across the Mediterranean, and to the oil-shipping lane across the Red Sea. For all these reasons, the Johnson administration increased military and economic assistance to Israel. Table 2 reveals that in 1966 Johnson gave Israel a total of $90 million in military assistance—the highest amount of aid given for any single year during the decade of the sixties.

The Johnson administration was responsive to Israel's ever increasing military needs even when the Israelis were the aggressors, using force to capture Arab land. During the 1967 War, the Israelis demonstrated their military superiority by defeating Egypt, Syria and Jordan. The Israeli occupation of the Sinai, Gaza, Golan Heights, and the West Bank of the Jordan River, including East Jerusalem, required additional military equipment to subjugate the Arab masses in the occupied territories. Johnson, instead of insisting on Israel's withdrawal from the Arab land as Eisenhower did in 1956, decided to meet Israel's new military requests by increasing U.S. assistance earmarked to Israel. In 1968, for instance, he gave Israel a total of $25 million in military assistance, an increase of 357 percent over the previous year. Shortly before leaving office, he sold Israel 50 Phantom jets as a replacement of French Mirages which President Charles de Gaulle withheld from Israel after the 1967 War. These long-range fighter-bombers supplied by the U.S. gave Israel a formidable offensive reinforcement and ensured the continuation of its air force superiority. As one observer put it: "The Phantoms changed the course of the war. . . . They were superior to any other airplane flown in the Middle East, particularly in range and firepower."[39]

Johnson's timely assistance helped Israel strike into the heartland of Egypt and consolidate its military control over the occupied Arab land. However, such an increase did not help restore peace in the war-torn Middle East. On the contrary, it aggravated the situation in the region, since it was only a matter of time before the Arabs were able to rebuild their armed forces and to embark on a military campaign to liberate their land. Furthermore, Johnson's tilt toward Israel did not serve U.S. interests in the Middle East; in fact, it provided the Soviet Union with new opportunities

TABLE 2
U.S. Military Assistance to Israel, 1949–1985
(Millions of Dollars)

	Loans	Grants	Total	Total in 1983 Dollars
1949–1952	—	—	—	—
1953–1961	0.9	—	0.9	3.0
1962	13.2	—	13.2	44.2
1963	13.3	—	13.3	44.0
1964	—	—	—	—
1965	12.9	—	12.9	41.4
1966	90	—	90	280.6
1967	7	—	7	21.2
1968	25	—	25	72.7
1969	85	—	85	234.7
1970	30	—	30	78.2
1971	545	—	545	1,360.8
1972	300	—	300	726.4
1973	307.5	—	307.5	700.7
1974	982.7	1,500	2,482.7	5,100.8
1975	200	100	300	564.5
1976	850	850	1,700	3,023.9
1977	500	500	1,000	1,669.7
1978	500	500	1,000	1,551.5
1979	2,700	1,300	4,000	5,587.9
1980	500	500	1,000	1,230.3
1981	900	500	1,400	1,557.0
1982	850	550	1,400	1,467.9
1983	950	750	1,700	1,700.0
1984	850	850	1,700	1,700.0
Total	11,212.5	7,900	19,112.5	28,761.4

Sources: U.S., Agency for International Development, Bureau for Program Policy and Coordination, *U.S. Overseas Loans and Grants and Assistance from International Organizations: Obligations and Loan Authorizations, July 1, 1945–June 30, 1971; July 1, 1945–September 30, 1977; July 1, 1945– September 30, 1979; and July 1, 1945–September 30, 1981. The New York Times,* August 10, 1982; *The Washington Post,* December 18, 1982. *The Mideast Observer in Washington,* April 15, 1983.

to penetrate the area by providing military aid to the Arab states, who were rearming themselves after the devastating defeat in the 1967 War.

The 1973 War: Nixon Rescues Israel

Johnson's increase of U.S. military assistance in 1968 was only the beginning of a steady escalation of American aid to Israel. When Richard M. Nixon assumed the presidency in 1969, he also substantially and steadily increased U.S. assistance to Israel. In 1969, U.S. military assistance reached $85 million—an increase of another 340 percent over the previous year. Such a sizeable increase came at a time when Israel continued its armed aggression on Egypt, Syria, Jordan and Lebanon. Israel's air raids continuously struck deep over Egyptian territory—a situation that served mainly to accelerate Soviet involvement in the region. In January 1970, for example, Egypt's Gamal Abdel Nasser made a secret four-day trip to Moscow to plead for better defensive weapons in the face of Israel's daily bombing of Egypt's major cities. The Soviet Union, in response, agreed to provide Egypt with a new missile defense system to deter the Israelis from continuing their air strikes. Soviet technicians began training Egyptian personnel to man these missile bases and Soviet pilots provided protective air coverage over Egypt's interior against Israeli air strikes in Cairo and other cities.[40]

The neutralization of Israel's air superiority was frustrating to both Israel and the U.S.; they did not wish to see the military balance in the region tip in the Arab favor since this might result not only in more U.S. military assistance to Israel but, potentially too, in greater need for American military intervention in the Middle East.

Under these circumstances, U.S. Secretary of State William Rogers proposed in June 1970 a limited cease-fire between Israel, Egypt, and Jordan in an attempt to clear the way for indirect talks to reach a political solution for the Arab-Israeli conflict. He also called on these governments to accept publicly the U.N. Security Council Resolution 242 of November 22, 1967 as the basis for peace talks. This Resolution called for Israeli withdrawal from the occupied Arab territories and a pledge by the parties concerned to seek a permanent settlement. He also suggested that the mission of U.N. special envoy Gunnar Jarring be resumed to search for a solution.

Egypt and Jordan first announced their unconditional acceptance of the Rogers proposals. Israel, on the other hand, was cool to the American initiatives, largely because it had repeatedly refused to accept the Security

Council Resolution 242 of 1967, particularly about Israel's obligation to withdraw from the occupied Arab land. Yet, in the face of the Arab acceptance, outright rejection would put Israel in an awkward position with the Nixon administration, which might find it difficult to continue arms shipments to Israel. Under U.S. pressure, Israel finally accepted the broad outlines of the Rogers plan;[41] it did so, however, only after it had received assurances from Nixon that the arms balance in the Middle East would be maintained and that Israel would not have to withdraw from the occupied territories without first obtaining a permanent settlement.

To fulfill his pledge to help Israel maintain its military superiority, Nixon once again sharply increased U.S. military assistance to Israel. In 1971, Israel received a total of $545 million in U.S. military assistance in contrast to only $30 million in the previous year. It seems that the U.S. paid a high price for Israel's acceptance of the Rogers plan, even though Israel had no intention of relinquishing its control over the occupied territories. This was evident in the failure of the Jarring mission to convince Israel to trade occupied Arab land for security. The cease-fire Rogers had arranged was short-lived, since Israel insisted that its troops would move only to secure, recognized and agreed boundaries that would necessarily include large tracts of the Arab land. Furthermore, Israel continued to erect new Jewish settlements in the occupied land as a step toward future annexation. Although these settlements have been a thorny issue between the U.S. and Israel, Washington has failed to translate its verbal criticism into policy action to pressure the Israelis to cease building new settlements. Despite world-wide condemnation of the settlements, the U.S. has continued to provide Israel with military and economic assistance, which helps Israel to impose its military control over the occupied Arab land.

The decade of the seventies witnessed a continued escalation of U.S. military assistance to Israel. The largest increase came in the aftermath of the Ramadan War of 1973. At the outset of the war, Egyptian troops successfully crossed the Suez Canal and crushed the Bar Lev line of defense in the Sinai, and the Syrians crossed the Allon line in the Golan Heights. When the Arabs were about to win the duel, Nixon came to the rescue of Israel in an unprecedented manner. He put U.S. troops in the area on a military alert and, further, airlifted critical military hardware to Israel to help turn the tide in favor of Israel. This U.S. massive airlift of military equipment in the early days of the fighting was decisive to the outcome. The Nixon stance during the 1973 War made it clear that the Arabs were in no position to win a war against Israel because the U.S. was ready to devote tremendous resources to preventing Israel's defeat.

It should be noted that the U.S. did so at a high cost. The Nixon administration had to dip into its own reserves to meet Israel's military needs, thus jeopardizing U.S. national security for the sake of helping Israel. It also turned out that the U.S. sacrificed its own economic well-being by siding with Israel; the Arab oil-producing countries imposed an oil embargo against the U.S., which precipitated the energy crisis and a subsequent escalation of oil prices, shaking the foundations of Western economies. General Ira C. Eaker, who commanded Allied Air Forces in the Mediterranean in World War II, commented that the 1973 War: "cost this country at least $4 billion. It used up scarce reserves of weapons and supplies and lost the critical Arab oil. General Motors, during the embargo, laid off 65,000 workers and put 5,700 more on temporary furlough, and the entire U.S. economy was affected inasmuch as this move had repercussions on GM's 13,000 dealers and 45,000 suppliers. There was hardly a company or person in the U.S. who did not suffer in some way from the shortage of materials, rising costs or even unemployment stemming from the embargo. Completely forgotten, too, was the cost to the United States and Europe of the closing of the (Suez) Canal from 1967 to 1975, well over $10 billion."[42]

In the aftermath of the Ramadan War, the Nixon administration determined to give Israel a qualitative and technological edge over its Arab neighbors, again increased military assistance to Israel. Republican officals believed that the route to peace lay in Israel's ability to wage war. Thus, U.S. military assistance to Israel increased significantly in 1974, to a record high of $2.5 billion, twice as much as Israel had received in U.S. military aid for the whole period between 1949 and 1972. It is important to note that $1.5 billion out of the $2.5 billion were given as grants—a practice that was introduced by Nixon for the first time in the history of U.S. military assistance to Israel. In fact, the year 1974 marked the beginning of a sizeable increase in the amount of U.S. military aid to Israel and a growing emphasis on grants.

The Nixon administration sought to use this huge military aid as an incentive to persuade the Israelis to work with the U.S. on a temporary settlement in the Middle East as a step toward a permanent solution to the long-standing Arab-Israeli conflict. American policy-planners saw two alternatives in the Middle East situation: either an endless war would continue, with the possibility of an eventual confrontation between the U.S. and the Soviet Union or, instead, the U.S. must search for a permanent solution. They chose to try the latter approach. Secretary of State Henry A. Kissinger formulated a new policy toward the Middle East. Taking advantage of the detente between Washington and Moscow, he sought to find a political solution to the Arab-Israeli conflict—a solution that circumvented the crux of the problem, however. He ignored the Palestinian yearning for self-determination; nor was he willing to deal with the PLO, recognized as the legitimate representative of the Palestinian people by the U.N., the League of Arab States, the Non-Aligned Movement, the Organization of African Unity and the Islamic Conference. Instead, Kissinger sought to reach a temporary arrangement between Egypt, Syria and Israel to pave the way for new efforts to find a peaceful solution. His "shuttle diplomacy" eventually resulted in the conclusion of the Disengagement Agreements on the Sinai. His diplomatic efforts also persuaded Egypt's Anwar El-Sadat to sever relations with the Soviet Union and to establish closer ties with the U.S. Such a development weakened the military capabilities of the Arab frontline states as Sadat became more interested in seeking a negotiated settlement for the Middle Eastern conflict. It also removed any immediate threat to Israel, which was receiving extensive military aid during this time.

The resignation of Nixon did not affect the flow of U.S. aid to Israel, in part because Kissinger was retained as Secretary of State under the new President. Gerald Ford, with his sights set on the 1976 election, increased aid to Israel to rally the Jewish vote behind his bid for the presidency. In 1976, for example, Israel received $1.5 billion in U.S. military assistance in contrast to $300 million the year before. This five-fold increase in U.S. military assistance was in response to Israel's pleas for more aid to keep up with the race for arms in the Middle East. The initial goal of the race was the replacement of weapons destroyed during the 1973 War. "But this seems to have triggered a cycle of action and reaction in which each side now strives to better the arsenal of the other. As a result, both sides are not only stronger than before the October War but are also acquiring some of the world's most sophisticated weaponry."[43] The U.S. has been responsible for fueling the arms race in the Middle East by providing Israel with massive military assistance, including huge amounts in grants, in an effort to match part of Arab defense increases. A recent study reveals that "U.S. supply of assistance is positively correlated with Arab defense outlays and negatively correlated with Israel's gross national product growth."[44] It concludes that "the Arabs appear to be more reactive to Israeli military expenditures than vice versa." In addition, "the Arabs allocate, at the margin, a somewhat lesser increment of income growth to defense."[45]

Ford, like his predecessors, was interested in increasing Israel's ability to deal with whatever threats it faced. For this reason, he increased the level of U.S. military assistance to help Israel meet the challenges in the Middle East.

The PLO had moved its headquarters to Beirut and set up bases in southern Lebanon. When the civil war broke out in Lebanon in 1976, the PLO sided with the progressive Lebanese movement, which favors revision of Lebanon's confessional governmental system, while Israel threw its weight behind the isolationist forces. This situation required prompt action by the U.S. to prevent a victory by the progressive elements. Ford, whose war powers were crippled by Congress, could not convince congressional leaders to get the U.S. directly involved in the Lebanese crisis. Instead, he decided to increase American military aid to Israel, thus enabling Israel to intervene in Lebanon's internal affairs. Israel provided weapons and logistical support to the isolationist Maronite Phalangists; carried out massive air strikes against the Lebanese and Palestinian civilian centers; and later crossed the borders into southern Lebanon and intervened militarily to ensure victory by the fascist forces. Israel's objective was to create the proper conditions to crush the Palestinian armed struggle, to defeat the Lebanese progressive forces, and to ensure Maronite Phalangist control and domination in Lebanon.

Camp David: More Arms Transfers

The same stance continued under President Jimmy Carter, who was sympathetic to Israel's position on security because of the continuing Lebanese crisis and the rising tension between Israel and the PLO. For this reason, he maintained the high level of U.S. military assistance which, with the exception of 1979, amounted to one billion dollars a year. The bulk of the increased assistance came in a single year—1979—during which U.S. military assistance reached a record-breaking high point of $4 billion. This substantial increase was in fact a reward to Israel for signing the Camp David Accords, in which Israel agreed to withdraw from the occupied Sinai over a three-year period and to grant "autonomy" to the Palestinians in the West Bank and Gaza.[46] To facilitate Israeli acceptance of the Accords, the Carter administration agreed to increase the volume of U.S. military assistance to Israel, to finance the construction of new military bases and airports in the Negev Desert, and to supply Israel with new weaponry to ensure the continuation of Israel's military advantage in the region.

Although Israel agreed to a five-year transition period of Palestinian "autonomy" on the West Bank and Gaza under the Camp David Accords, no progress has been made in the "autonomy talks." This is primarily because Begin, who resigned as Prime Minister in September 1983, saw "autonomy" as a temporary arrangement leading to an Israeli assertion of sovereignty. He had always insisted that these territories are part of the Biblical land of Israel. He therefore had no plan to relinquish Israel's control over them.[47] Israel also has refused to include the 100,000 Palestinians living in East Jerusalem in the "autonomy plan." Having annexed East Jerusalem after the 1967 War, Israel does not intend to allow the Palestinians there to participate in the autonomous council. Furthermore, Israel does not agree to granting voting rights to the Palestinians except for local matters. Consequently, Israel narrowly interprets "autonomy" to mean that the Israeli government would retain control over the "autonomous council," which it wants to appoint. Such a council would have some "administrative functions" but no legislative powers, with the Israeli cabinet holding a veto power on administrative decisions and foreign affairs. Egypt, on the other hand, has more liberally interpreted autonomy, seeing it as a phase leading to self-determination by all Palestinians in the occupied territories, including East Jerusalem, preparatory to independence.[48] Egypt also advocates the establishment of an elected parliamentary-type body of 50 members empowered to enact legislation. Due to these fundamental differences, Egypt and Israel are far from reaching an agreement on how to organize the autonomous body, much less on the council's size and on its specific functions.

Despite Israel's failure to live up to the commitments made in the Camp David Accords, Carter saw no reason to use U.S. leverage with Israel to get Begin to grant autonomy to the Palestinians in the West Bank and Gaza. On the contrary, his administration continued business-as-usual with the Israeli government. It continued to provide Israel with military assistance to beef up its ability to impose its military control over the occupied land, despite Israel's record of human rights violations[49]—an issue that the Carter administration had espoused as a cornerstone of U.S. foreign policy.

Reagan and Israel's Invasion of Lebanon

When Ronald Reagan assumed the presidency in 1981, there was a noticeable improvement in U.S.-Israel relations. Reagan's conservatism led to the re-emergence of the cold-war rivalry and once again made the Middle East a pawn in the East-West conflict. U.S.-Middle Eastern policy has become an integral part of a global strategy to "establish restraints on Soviet behavior."[50] Reagan's plan for a "strategic consensus" of anti-communist states in the Middle East thus brought him closer to Israel and put him at arm's-distance from the Camp David Accords.

At the beginning, Reagan showed little or no interest at all in the autonomy talks—which had been on-again off-again because of Israel's intransigence. He increased U.S. military assistance to Israel, however, reaching a total of $1.4 billion in 1981 and again in 1982. In addition, Israel was forgiven repayment of $500 million in 1981 and $550 million in 1982, respectively. Reagan also accepted Begin's proposals for a military link with the U.S. On November 30, 1981, the U.S. signed with Israel a memorandum on strategic cooperation and agreed to assist Israel to build up its arms industries. This was alleged to be part of Reagan's plan to combat military threats by the Soviet Union and its allies in the Middle East. The U.S. also was planning joint American-Israeli naval and air maneuvers in the eastern Mediterranean and the prepositioning of U.S. supplies in Israel. The Reagan administration also agreed to give serious consideration to the following Israeli requests: (1) authorize the U.S. Defense Department to purchase military equipment from Israel up to $200 million a year; (2) allow Israel to use U.S. military assistance funds to buy from its domestic arms industries rather than from U.S. firms; and (3) permit other nations receiving U.S. military aid to use part of their funds to purchase equipment and services from Israel.[51]

This agreement was a victory for the Israeli government, since it signified a special relationship with the U.S. Begin hoped that it could lead to an increase in military cooperation between the U.S. and Israel. The Reagan administration, however, decided to suspend the strategic cooperation agreement 18 days later, because of Israel's annexation of the Golan Heights. On December 14, the Israeli Knesset voted to extend Israeli law to the Golan Heights, which Israel had occupied since 1967. This move was a virtual annexation of the territory—an action that was declared "null and void" by the U.S. and the U.N. Security Council.[52]

The Republican administration was angered by Israel's decision to annex the Golan Heights. Dean Fischer, State Department spokesman, stated that "The Israeli action was taken with no advance notice . . . We are particularly disappointed that the government of Israel took this action just as we were facing a serious political crisis in Poland and only a few weeks after we signed a memorandum of understanding on strategic cooperation." Fisher added that "The spirit of that agreement obliged each party to take into consideration in its decisions the implications for the broad policy concerns of the other. We do not believe that this spirit was upheld in the case of Israel's decision on the Golan."[53] He stressed the U.S. position that the final status of the Golan Heights can only be determined through negotiations between Israel and Syria based upon U.N. Security Council Resolutions 242 and 338.

U.S.-Israeli relations deteriorated further in the aftermath of Israel's invasion of Lebanon in the summer of 1982. The widespread Israeli use of U.S.-made cluster bombs against Lebanese and Palestinian civilians— which violated the terms of U.S. agreements with Israel—led Reagan to place a ban on the shipment of such weapons to Israel. Relations have been further strained as a result of the slaughter of hundreds of Palestinian refugees at the Sabra and Shatila camps in West Beirut in September 1982. American officials have blamed Israel for the Palestinian massacres because Israeli Defense Minister Ariel Sharon had ordered his troops, which were guarding the camps, to allow the Phalangist militiamen to enter the grounds; this was done even though, a short time earlier, Sharon had expressed concern that the Christian militia would massacre Palestinians.[54]

The massacres of Palestinian civilians have presented a moral and legal dilemma for the U.S., whose special envoy Philip C. Habib had guaranteed the safety of Palestinians in Beirut after the PLO pullout.[55] Furthermore, the massacres led many Americans to question the extent to which the U.S. should be willing to tolerate Begin's military ventures in implementing his territorial expansionist scheme to create Greater Israel.

To put the brakes on future Zionist plans for the annexation of the West Bank, Reagan has come up with a new initiative to find a peaceful solution to the Arab-Israeli conflict. In September 1982 Reagan called for a "fresh start" in the long-drawn-out Middle East peace talks. He called for a freeze on Jewish settlements in the occupied land and came out in favor of "full autonomy" for the West Bank and Gaza in association with Jordan. He recommended that the future of Jerusalem should be determined through negotiations, although he favored having the city remain undivided. He also expressed a strong commitment to Israel's "security."[56]

Arab reaction to Reagan's initiative was favorable. Although Reagan did not advocate the establishment of a Palestinian state, they saw that his plan had several merits. Arab governments thus expressed an interest in continuing a dialogue with the U.S. to seek a permanent settlement for the war-torn Middle East. Israel, on the other hand, rejected Reagan's proposals, since it did not agree with Begin's plan to incorporate the West Bank and Gaza into Israel.[57] Despite the negative Israeli reaction, Reagan continued efforts to convince the Israeli government to trade occupied Arab land for peace in the region.

The Israeli government has been able to ignore U.S. overtures because of past American promises not to link military and economic assistance to Israel to political issues such as Reagan's peace initiative[58] or his proposed freeze on new Jewish settlements in the occupied West Bank. Thus, the U.S. failure to use foreign aid as a means to pressure Israel to trade occupied land for security has been the reason for the U.S.'s inability to deliver the pledges made in the Camp David Accords. As it stands now, the U.S. has only succeeded in concluding a peace treaty between Egypt and Israel—a step that resulted in weakening the Arabs militarily in their confrontation with Israel over return of their captured land. The Camp David Accords have placed American troops in the Sinai to serve as a buffer between Egypt and Israel, thus freeing the Israelis to concentrate their forces along their borders with other Arab states. The treaty has also given the Israelis an opportunity to initiate new ventures, such as their military intervention in Lebanon in 1982, without having to worry about Egypt's involvement on the side of the Arabs.

The U.S. has considerable leverage with Israel but Reagan's ability to use it has been undermined by congressional meddling in American foreign policy. An example was the Senate's rejection of the administration's appeal to keep aid to Israel at the same level—$1.7 billion in military assistance ($1.2 billion in loans and $500 million in grants) and $785 million in economic aid ($260 million in loans and $525 million in grants). In December the Senate, acting over the administration's objection, decided to make all of the economic assistance an outright grant and to transfer $350 million from military loans to grants. Thus, Israel will be exempted from paying back 50 percent of the military assistance, and 100 percent of the economic assistance.

The Senate's action dealt a potentially serious blow to the administration's effort to persuade Israel to stop placing obstacles in the way of the U.S.-sponsored talks for foreign troop withdrawal from Lebanon and to change its stance on Reagan's peace initiative. Congressional failure to support Reagan's policies in Lebanon and the Middle East encouraged Begin to ignore Reagan and to harden his position; apparently, he could rely on Israel's friends on Capitol Hill to provide him with substantial aid to carry out his expansionist plan regardless of whether it was in the national interest of the U.S. Administration sources have commented that "the

Senate's decision to defy Reagan's wishes at a time of strained U.S.-Israeli relations could have the psychological effect of convincing Israeli Prime Minister Menachem Begin that Reagan cannot count on congressional support if he takes a get-tough approach with Israel, and that Israel thus can ignore U.S. pressures with relative impunity."[59]

For fiscal year 1984, the Reagan administration requested $1.7 billion in military aid and $785 million in economic aid for Israel. This request came at a time when the Israeli invasion of Lebanon resulted in the death of 10,000 people, when 600,000 were made homeless and when U.S. Marines in Lebanon were being constantly harassed by the Israeli army. On March 14, the U.S. Marine Corp's Commandant General R. H. Barrow wrote Secretary of Defense Caspar Weinberger that, "It is evident to me, and the opinion of the U.S. commanders afloat and ashore, that the incidents between the Marines and the IDF are timed, orchestrated, and executed for obtuse Israeli political purposes." Israel's political goals in Lebanon were centered on the creation of a Lebanese puppet government which automatically will turn Lebanon into a market for Israeli goods. The generosity of the Reagan administration, nevertheless, was followed by an important policy decision. In a letter dispatched to Israel's Defense Minister in mid-April, Secretary of State George Shultz wrote that the three long-awaited licenses for parts and technology for the Lavi have been approved. In the same letter, Shultz revealed the reason for such approval when he stated, "I hope your meetings with Phil Habib will bring us closer to reaching an agreement (on an Israeli troop withdrawal from Lebanon)."[60] Despite all of this, Israel did not withdraw from Lebanon. The Congress, in an apparent move to compensate Israel for its losses in Lebanon, voted to increase Israel's share for fiscal year 1984 by $125 million and the grant allocation from $1.335 to $1.76 billion. The Congress also is expected to approve the same allocation for fiscal year 1985.

There must be a close collaboration between the White House and the Congress, if there is to be a chance for the U.S. to convince Israel to give a favorable response to Reagan's Mideast peace initiatives. The Israeli government must be convinced that it cannot expect support from Congress unless it shows a willingness to trade occupied Arab territory for peace. Under such circumstances, U.S. assistance could be used to pressure Israel to recognize that Reagan's proposals do represent, with modification, a fair basis for resuming negotiations. Whether the Reagan administration is willing to use Israel's dependence on U.S. aid as leverage is currently being debated in the White House and the State Department. The outcome will depend heavily on how much support Reagan can find in Congress and whether he will be able to convince American Jewish leaders to support his proposals for a permanent peace in the Middle East. If the administration moves firmly in dealing with Israel, there is a chance that a refined Reagan peace plan might succeed in getting the Arab-Israeli talks back on track to tackle the Palestinian issue, which so far has proved insurmountable.

2

U.S. ECONOMIC ASSISTANCE:
GOVERNMENT AND PRIVATE

United States economic involvement in Israel has been the backbone of Israel's continuing ability to deal with enormous economic problems resulting from a huge foreign debt, which has reached a record high of $21.5 billion in 1983; a decline in the GNP growth, which is now below 5 percent; and an annual rate of domestic inflation of 200 percent.[61] The primary reason underlying the deterioration of the Israeli economy is the diversion of domestic capital resources and manpower from development projects to military buildup. In 1980, for example, Israel spent 25 percent of its GNP and 14 percent of its total available resources on defense.[62] In addition, the costs of deploying Israeli troops and building of Jewish settlements in the occupied Arab territories as well as expenses related to the military invasions of Lebanon in 1978 and 1982 have added further constraints on Israel's economy.

Despite the rising military expenditures, Israel has been able to meet its expenses without heavy reliance on high-interest commercial loans, dipping into its foreign exchange reserves or causing economic depression. This is largely due to the U.S., which has always taken Israel's financial needs into account in determining appropriate aid levels.[63] Consequently, the U.S. has become the largest single source of capital inflow for Israel. Between 1949–1985, U.S. governmental assistance amounted to $30.7 billion. In addition, several other billions of dollars have been sent to Israel through unilateral transfers from American citizens and institutions as well as from the sale of Israel Bonds in the U.S.

Government Assistance

U.S. administrations—Democratic and Republican alike—have been responsive to Israel's financial needs in allocating U.S. economic and military assistance. To ease the financial burden of Israel's debt, American aid has been divided between grants and loans. Out of $28.1 billion assistance to Israel since 1949, the U.S. has given Israel $14.6 billion as outright grants, which Israel is under no obligation to pay back. In addition, Israel has routinely been granted long-grace and amortization periods on American loans, thus giving Israel a breathing period to deal with its balance-of-payment problems and to accelerate economic growth. A recent AID Report on the Israeli economy admitted that "Our economic and military assistance enables Israel to pay for weaponry, fuel and other civilian imports which it needs without overly heavy reliance on high cost commercial borrowing, depletion of its foreign exchange reserves, or economic depression."[64]

Over the years, Israel has grown heavily dependent on U.S. capital to meet its financial needs and to avert serious debt problems. This is particularly true because U.S. funds "involve no projects and, therefore, no AID supervisory staff. It's simply a check-writing operation."[65]

Table 3 shows that U.S. economic assistance has been substantial in volume and has steadily risen to meet Israel's ever increasing needs to deal with its ailing economy and to prevent its financial collapse. U.S. economic aid grew, for example, from as little as $15.7 million in 1967 to as much as $791.8 million in 1978. All in all, Israel has received a total of $8.9 billion in U.S. economic assistance since 1949, of which $6.7 billion have been given as outright grants.

Prior to the enactment of the Foreign Assistance Act of 1962, the U.S. gave more economic than military assistance. Eisenhower believed that it was not enough "to guard against the external military threats. . . . We must also move against those conditions exploited by subversive forces from within."[66] He placed greater importance on technical, economic and developmental projects.

Between 1953–1961, the U.S. concentrated on economic aid, giving Israel a total of $507.2 million, of which $258.9 million were given as grants. In addition, the Export-Import Bank supplied Israel with an additional $57 million in loans.

Table 3 reveals that there was a substantial increase in economic assistance to Israel in 1962. The Kennedy administration gave Israel a total of $80.2 million—the highest amount of aid given for any single year throughout the 1960s. The second largest increase came under the Johnson administration in 1968, during which economic assistance reached a total of $75.5 million. This came in the aftermath of the 1967 War and was intended to ease the financial strains on the Israeli budget caused by the cost of its military aggression. The 1968 aid package represented a five-fold increase in American economic aid over the year before.

TABLE 3
U.S. Economic Assistance to Israel, 1949–1985
(Millions of Dollars)

	Loans	Grants	Total	Total in 1983 Dollars
1949–1952	—	86.5	86.5	289.4
1953–1961	248.3	258.9	507.2	1,696.8
1962	73	7.2	80.2	268.3
1963	68.6	6	74.6	246.6
1964	32.2	4.8	37	120.6
1965	47.3	4.9	52.2	167.4
1966	35.8	0.9	36.7	114.4
1967	15.1	0.6	15.7	47.6
1968	75	0.5	75.5	219.6
1969	74.7	0.6	75.3	207.9
1970	51	0.4	51.4	134.0
1971	68.8	0.3	69.1	172.5
1972	53.8	50.4	104.2	252.3
1973	59.4	50.4	109.8	250.2
1974	—	51.5	51.5	105.8
1975	8.6	344.5	353.1	664.5
1976	268	525	793	1,410.6
1977	252	490	742	1,239.0
1978	266.8	525	791.8	1,228.5
1979	265.1	525	790.1	1,103.7
1980	261	525	786	967.0
1981	—	764	764	849.7
1982	—	806	806	845.1
1983	—	785	785	785.0
1984	—	910	910	910.0
Total	2,224.5	6,723.4	8,947.9	14,296.5

Sources: U.S., Agency for International Development, Bureau for Program Policy and Coordination, *U.S. Overseas Loans and Grants and Assistance from International Organizations: Obligations and Loan Authorizations, July 1, 1945–June 30, 1971; July 1, 1945–September 30, 1977; July 1, 1945– September 30, 1979; and July 1, 1945–September 30, 1981. The New York Times*, August 10, 1982; *The Washington Post*, December 18, 1982. *The Mideast Observer in Washington*, April 15, 1983.

The coming of the Nixon administration did not affect U.S. economic assistance to Israel. Nixon maintained the same high level of spending by providing Israel with $75.3 million in 1969. These high levels of aid in 1968 and 1969 were crucial to Israel, whose government was busy consolidating its military control over the land captured from Egypt, Syria and Jordan in the 1967 War. The Israeli occupation required additional funds from abroad, since Israel had fewer domestic revenue sources that were capable of meeting the high cost of subjugating more than one million Arab inhabitants in the Sinai, Gaza, the Golan Heights, and the West Bank, including East Jerusalem. The Nixon administration readily met Israel's financial needs by increasing U.S. economic assistance, reaching a new record high; it passed the $100-million mark in 1972 and again in 1973. These substantial increases were intended to help Israel overcome the increasing costs of the military occupation and a growing deficit in its balance-of-payments, which amounted to $3 billion in 1975 alone. Washington spared no effort to assist Israel in dealing with the deficit and in financing its development plans without heavy reliance on high-interest commercial loans and without slipping into economic recession.

Nixon's resignation had no negative effect on the flow of aid to Israel. In fact, in 1975, Israel received a total of $353.1 million in economic assistance, compared to only $51.5 million the year before. This represented a seven-fold increase over the previous year; it was, up until then, the largest amount of economic aid Israel had yet received from the U.S. since its inception in 1948. It also marked a sharp escalation in the volume of U.S. economic assistance. In the following year, Ford increased the economic assistance to Israel two-fold, reaching a total of $793 million. This also set up a precedent for substantial economic aid to Israel—a level that has been maintained by both Carter and Reagan. Israel received between $742 million and $792 million annually during the Carter years. Similarly, Reagan gave Israel $764 million in economic assistance in 1981 and $806 million in 1982.

Before Israel's invasion of Lebanon in summer 1982, Reagan asked Congress to allocate $785 million in economic assistance and $1.7 billion in military aid to Israel in the 1983 budget. The Senate, however, decided in December 1982 to shift $260 million in economic assistance from loans to grants and to transfer $250 million from military loans to grants. Senator Mark O. Hatfield (R-Ore.) expressed his concern that, by this action, the Senate "is sending a signal that it supports the invasion and continued occupation of Lebanon. . . . It is very difficult to justify (the U.S.) being the largest arms peddler in the world when we are cutting all these domestic programs."[67]

The Reagan administration was opposed to the transfer in fiscal 1983 because of Israel's delaying tactics in getting the talks on troop withdrawal from Lebanon off the ground as well as the outright rejection of Reagan's proposals for a settlement for the Arab-Israeli conflict. Kenneth W. Dam, Deputy Secretary of State, stated that the increase of outright grants to Israel would "imperil the strenuous effort we are making to find a settlement in Lebanon and to make progress in the broader peace process."[68] It is believed that such an increase will anger Arab states and endanger Reagan's peace initiative. It would also take limited foreign aid funds away from "other U.S. friends and allies, including Spain, Portugal, Turkey and Pakistan,"[69] Dam said.

For the fiscal year 1984, the Reagan administration requested $785 million in grants for economic assistance. The Congress, however, approved $910 million.

It is interesting to note the configuration of loans and grants in the allocation of U.S. economic assistance. Between 1962-1971, most American economic aid was given as loans that obligated Israel to pay the funds back. The amount in grants was kept at a minimal level. For example, between 1966-1971, grants amounted to less than one million dollars in any given year.

Since 1972, grants have been sharply increased in response to Israel's requests for more American aid to offset its huge external deficit, which reached $4.6 billion in 1975, $3.9 billion in 1977 and $5.4 billion in 1979, respectively.[70] Since Israel cannot meet its financial obligations without foreign debts, the U.S. has come to the rescue in order to uphold the Israeli economy. This has resulted in a sharp increase in the volume of U.S. economic assistance as well as a dramatic increase in the amount that is given as grants. This trend began under the Nixon administration and has continued under his Republican and Democratic successors. In 1972 and 1973, 48 percent and 46 percent, respectively, of the U.S. economic assistance was given as outright grants. In the following year, in the aftermath of the 1973 War, the entire package of economic aid was given in the form of grants. In 1975, Israel received a total of $353.1 million from the U.S., of which 97.5 percent was given as grants. In the following years, the same trend continued, with grants always far exceeding the loans under both the

Ford and the Carter administrations. From fiscal year 1981 through fiscal
year 1984, the Reagan administration and Congress, however, again gave
Israel the total package of $3.3 billion as grants.

The year 1975 marked the beginning of a sizeable increase in the
amount of U.S. economic assistance to Israel and of a growing emphasis on
grants. The long-term U.S. objective is to prevent the shaky Israeli economy from collapse—an economy that has been overburdened by the military expenditures resulting from Israel's continued occupation of the land
captured from neighboring Arab states in the 1967 War. The Israeli economy has been further strained by Israel's invasion of Lebanon in 1978 and
1982. In addition, the Israeli government has been spending approximately
$100 million a year to erect Jewish settlements in the occupied West Bank
as a preparatory step toward its annexation. Its plan is to resettle 100,000
Jews in the West Bank by 1985, as a way to facilitate its scheme to create
Greater Israel. It was recently reported that the Israeli government has been
using U.S. aid to finance the construction of settlements in the West Bank
and to encourage the Israelis to move to the new settlements by offering
financial rewards.[71]

Although the settlement issue has caused disagreement between the
U.S. and Israel, the U.S. administrations, aside from verbal criticism, have
not initiated any measures to ensure that U.S. funds are not spent on
settlements in the occupied Arab land. Rather, U.S. economic assistance
has made it possible for the Zionists to carry out their colonial plan for the
West Bank without relying solely on Israel's domestic resources. Consequently, it is not enough for the Reagan administration to secure a promise
from the Israeli government that American aid will not be used to finance
Jewish settlements in the occupied land. The Israelis have been able to
divert some of their domestic resources to finance these settlements and,
instead, to use U.S. assistance to cover the cost of economic projects inside
Israel that, otherwise, would have been funded by their domestic revenue
sources.

Private Assistance

U.S. private assistance given as charitable dollars have played a significant role in relieving pressure on the Israeli economy, which has grown
accustomed to relying heavily on U.S. government and private assistance.
Tax-free, tax-deductible contributions, large in volume, have become part
and parcel of the Israeli national budget, giving the government flexibility

in shifting budget allocations. Private American funds have been used, especially, to cover areas that are not provided for by U.S. governmental loans and grants. Thus, Israel has been able to finance some development projects without dipping into its scarce domestic resources, which have been diverted to cover its huge military expenditures.

Private American assistance is obtained from three major sources: (1) private institutions; (2) private individuals; and (3) the sale of Israel Bonds. Over the years, these sources have generated billions of dollars for Israel from the prosperous American Jewish community and, to a lesser extent, from non-Jewish sources. Between 1948–1977, these sources raised $10.8 billion (15 billion in 1983 U.S. dollars) for Israel: Private institutions accounted for $4.3 billion, private individuals for $3.3 billion, and the purchase of Israel Bonds for $3.2 billion.[72] It should be noted that such assistance is the largest ever collected from private sources in any country. In fact, American individual transfers and the purchase of Israel Bonds accounted for 75 percent of all such foreign transfers and purchases among all countries during that period.[73]

The U.S. government has facilitated the task of soliciting private funds for Israel. One example is that the sale of Israel Bonds is not subject to the Interest Equalization Tax, which is applied to other foreign securities.[74] Another is that the U.S. Internal Revenue Service (IRS) has approved the non-profit charitable status of several Jewish and Zionist organizations, chiefly among them, the United Jewish Appeal (UJA). The UJA and many others are active in fund-raising to sustain Israel and to prevent its ailing economy from collapsing.

The funds generated through these organizations are not spent solely on humanitarian projects in Israel but on political and/or governmental functions as well. A good example is the Jewish Agency, receiving a great share of its revenue from the UJA, which has been given tremendous power through an agreement signed with the Israeli government in 1954. This agreement, known as the "Covenant," defines the functions of the Jewish Agency in areas of immigration, agriculture, investment, cultural activities, and finance—some of which are governmental functions. The Jewish Agency, however, assumes such responsibilities and operates as a state-within-a-state by acting as the international arm of the Israeli government with a broad spectrum of domestic activities.

Ordinarily, amounts collected in the U.S. are put at the disposal of the Jewish Agency, which, in turn, uses the funds to finance various projects.

During the period between 1920–1970, the Agency carried out the following projects:[75]

Name of Project	Cost in $M
Immigration and Absorption	$ 573.0
Health Service	77.1
Education	74.6
Youth Aliyah	156.2
Immigrant Housing	432.5
Agricultural Settlement	945.8
Educational Activities	294.2
Overseas Operations	160.5
Various Activities	301.6
Total	$3015.5

The 1954 Covenant also calls for "taxing the Diaspora." The taxing of American Jews, which is conducted by the United Jewish Appeal (UJA), is treated by the IRS as similar in function to that of the Easter Seal and the Red Cross and, therefore, is considered charitable and tax-deductible.

The Zionists argue that American Jews have the "collective duty" to "assist the state of Israel" in its major concerns, such as colonization, economic development, and national security.[76] Thus, the "American Jewish community," although it has chosen not to immigrate, is expected, instead, to contribute generously to uphold the Israeli economy and to help it defer some of the costs of military buildup and economic development.

Another important function of the Jewish Agency is to facilitate Jewish immigration into Israel. Until the 1967 War, the Israeli government covered fifty percent of the cost of the immigration program to attract new settlers; after 1967, the Agency has absorbed more than two-thirds of these costs. The Jewish Agency, with an annual budget of $500 million, has to rely heavily on contributions from world Jewry. American Jews have always been responsive to the Agency's appeals and have contributed generously to support efforts to resettle Jewish migrants in Israel. For example, between 1972–1978, Americans donated to Israel $177.5 million for immigration purposes.

Over the decades, the Jewish Agency has been able to finance the resettlement of Jews in Israel on a large scale, spending approximately $17,000 per family. Between 1967–1974, the Agency spent a total of $2.1 billion to cover the expenses of settling 205,000 people in Israel.[77]

Overall, the immigrants who were accommodated by the Jewish Agency between 1948–1970 totalled 1,399,112 people.[78] Also, the Agency has been able to attract and accommodate in Israel 3,000 skilled American technicians and scientists. "This pool of technical talent is emerging as one of Israel's most important national assets for developing (its) long-range potential."[79]

The donations of individuals and private institutions as well as the sale of Israel Bonds are essential to sustain the Zionist state and to help accelerate its economic development. The purchase of Israel Bonds is not made purely on sound business grounds but rather on political and emotional considerations. An example was the Teamster's decision in 1973 to invest $26 million of its pension, health and welfare funds in Israel Bonds. The 5.5 percent return on Israel Bonds due in twenty years was far below the interest rate available in the U.S. bonds at that time. Since the U.S. bonds' return was 6.9 percent annual yield, the union's pension funds lost $7.3 million over the twenty-year period based on the differences between the annual return of both bonds.[80] It is questionable financial judgment that union management decided to invest in Israel Bonds rather than the U.S. bonds, despite the sizeable loss in revenue in the long run.

The Zionist rationale behind purchasing Israel Bonds is to involve Diaspora Jews in building, maintaining, and now expanding, the Zionist state. These collections existed from Herzl's time — though not the Bonds. Private American sources are expected to have supplied Israel with approximately $14 billion between 1949 and 1985. These huge sums have helped Israel overcome the costs of meeting the challenges of sustaining a moderate rate of economic growth despite adverse conditions stemming from a mounting foreign debt and huge military expenditures. It can be concluded that the large amount of money channeled by the American Jewish and Zionist organizations and by the purchase of Israel Bonds indicates the degree of Israel's dependence on the financial support from U.S. citizens and institutions, not to mention the huge subsidy the U.S. government gives to Israel year in and year out.

There is also a legal question resulting from the official link between the Israeli government and U.S. Zionist and Jewish organizations such as the UJA. Their charitable, tax-deductible status is in question due to the political nature of their activities and their financial involvement in functions that are supposedly governmental operations, such as funding new Israeli settlements in the occupied Arab land and promoting and financing Jewish immigration to Israel. These activities are not in accordance with the spirit and letter of U.S. law, which permits tax exemption only for humanitarian and charitable activities. The U.S. failure to enforce its own law raises serious questions about U.S. complicity with Israel and about the U.S. desire to search for a just solution for the Question of Palestine.

American Economic Involvement in Israel

Over the decades, Israel has needed foreign capital to stimulate economic growth. It has encouraged foreign—particularly American—investment because it has suffered from a shortage of local capital and of the capital equipment needed for economic development. The Israeli strategy is that, through energetic efforts of American and European investors, the general level of economic activity can be accelerated. This, in turn, can lead to greater exports and greater foreign exchange earnings.

With this in mind, Israel concluded a treaty with the U.S. in June 1965, which was intended to eliminate the system of double taxation which had previously hampered Israel's efforts to attract substantial U.S. investment. Under this agreement, Israel pledged to provide American corporations with:[81]

- deductions on industrial assets;
- relief on taxation of income and company's profits;
- exemption from Israeli taxation, provided that such a company does not have a permanent establishment in Israel;
- limitation of Israeli taxation on interest derived from sources within Israel to 15 percent;
- limitation on taxation of dividends derived within Israel to 25 percent of the gross amount of the dividends actually distributed; and
- credit of 25 percent to "eligible corporations" of U.S. origin which invest in Israel.

The U.S., in return, committed itself to giving a credit against U.S. taxes to American firms which invest in Israel as well as to granting a tax deferment when such companies provide Israel with technical assistance.

Between 1969 and 1972, Israel initiated several new policies to encourage the flow of American and foreign capital into the Israeli economy. In June 1969, for instance, it agreed to give tax concessions on reinvested profits; a tax incentive for mergers and acquisitions, designed to promote industrial groupings; and a provision for accelerated depreciation. Other measures attempted to tackle the problems of red tape that had placed roadblocks in the way of foreign investment. Thus, a single administrative unit—the Investment Authority—was established to handle all initial transactions.

These policies and facilities did not produce fruitful results. The Israeli system of taxation continued to discourage the flow of foreign capital into Israel. Consequently, a new policy was adopted in 1975 that dealt exclusively with taxes. The following concessions were made for foreign investors: (1) company profit taxes were to be cut down from 42 percent to 40 percent; and (2) the capital gain tax was reduced to 10 percent.[82]

This policy failed to deal with the problem of taxation on a broad basis, however. Many tax provisions were left intact that put the credibility of the new policy in question. For instance, the total tax burden was increased from 59.4 percent to 61 percent. The undistributed profit of industrial enterprises was to be taxed by 28 percent and gradually would reach 35 percent, as opposed to 15 percent, previously. Future profit would be taxed 40 percent plus 15 percent for income tax, to be raised to 35 percent in 1977.[83] Such a taxation system proved to be a continuing obstacle to foreign investment.

To deal with these problems, the Israeli government decided in 1977 to (1) decontrol foreign exchange; (2) ease the credit squeeze; (3) float the Israeli currency; and (4) remove subsidies of basic commodities.[84] Having initiated these new regulations, Israel turned to her major trading partners and their multinational corporations in her quest for substantial amounts of foreign capital. She found a sympathetic response from American firms, whose government had not opposed the flow of capital and technology into Israel. These efforts resulted in a sizeable increase in private U.S. investment in Israel, which has come to play a major role in the Israeli economic boom since 1967; it now accounts for 55 percent of total foreign investment in Israel.[85]

Israel has developed strong bonds of cooperation with the American business community despite some serious economic disadvantages of investment in Israel. Israel, first of all, has a very small market, with a population of only 3.5 million people. Secondly, American firms doing business with Israel are boycotted by Arab states and are not allowed to operate in the Arab world, whose population collectively exceeds 140 million. This means a potential loss of business for American companies since the Arab markets—with a large purchasing power—are closed as long as these corporations have operations in Israel.

Despite these shortcomings, the Israeli government has succeeded in attracting U.S. business. The major attractions for American investors appear to be strong sentiment on the part of the members of the American—particularly Jewish—business community for helping Israel sustain its economy, which has "experienced a period of severe balance of payments difficulties, . . . slack demand for imports in OECD countries, and the need to rearm and modernize Israeli defense forces."[86] Consequently, Israel has had no problem in attracting a continuing flow of American and other foreign capital. Israel has thus become heavily dependent on American and foreign capital to deal with stagnant growth, low productivity, a triple-digit inflation plus a worsening balance-of-payments deficit and a mounting foreign debt.

To increase the volume of foreign private investment, the Israeli government has often appealed to the Jewish business community in the U.S. and elsewhere to advise it "on necessary steps in order to expand the Israeli economy and to end Israel's dependence on Jewish contributions." The first conference was held in 1967 and identified Israel's economic ills as follows: (1) high taxes; (2) red tape; (3) limitless bureaucracy; (4) government competition with free enterprise; and (5) powerful and vested local interest groups, especially labor unions.[87]

In 1968, a second conference was convened in Jerusalem, where 500 Jewish businessmen (with known wealth of $4 billion) participated and pledged to:[88]

- develop a market for Israeli goods in their country of citizenship;
- mobilize Jewish and non-Jewish investment in their countries for the production and marketing of Israeli goods;
- facilitate subcontracts abroad for Israeli manufacturers;
- arrange for patents, know-how and management agreements with Israeli undertakings;
- help Israel export engineering, scientific and technological services;
- recruit able managerial, merchandising and technological staff for Israeli enterprises; and
- make arrangements in their own and with other enterprises abroad for on-the-job training of Israeli management and technological personnel.

The conference also recommended that Israel should make basic changes in its economic climate, i.e. eliminate the ills suggested by the 1967 conference in order to attract foreign investment.

In 1973, a third and final conference took place in Jerusalem. The conference was attended by 1000 businessmen of which 900 were Jews. Henry Ford, who is a gentile, summed up the recommendations of the conference by stating, "Israel needed bigger business. The key to increasing Israeli exports was a shift from enterprises producing in small quantities at high cost for local markets to ventures capable of producing at a high volume and low cost for the world market."[89]

This conference series ended in part because the Israeli government was unwilling to follow such recommendations and in part because the Investment Corporation set up during the second conference went bankrupt. Israel's failure to accept such recommendations was also based on ideological grounds; the recommendations would require Israel to put an emphasis on mass production rather than on land settlement and/or development; the Moshav and Kibbutz factions strongly advocate the latter goals. Any drastic shift of emphasis will inevitably antagonize these groups. Another reason for Israel's refusal to implement the recommendations is its desire to maintain full employment, thus accepting a high economic cost rather than facing a mounting labor unrest that would shake the foundations of the Israeli economy.

American Investment

In general, American investment has played a significant role in Israel's economic development, contributing to the quantitative growth of the economy in general and of industry in particular.

(A) Direct Government Investment in Israel

Direct government investment in Israel is channeled through the financing and/or participation of the U.S. government in Israeli projects. Largely, this financial involvement is accomplished through U.S. loans provided to the Israeli government and institutions for the sole purpose of undertaking specific projects. Between 1966 and 1974, the U.S. government invested a total of $481.5 million in Israel for a total of 56 projects. These projects were diversified, ranging from construction of university buildings to desalinization power plants. The terms of American loans to Israel are typically very generous: interest rates range from .75 percent to 4 percent and periods of repayment are from 17 months to 40 years. Between 1975 and 1977, the Export-Import Bank provided Israel with $270 million at a 2 percent interest rate payable over a period of 40 years.[90] America's declared purpose behind such investments is to promote Israel's economic growth and political stability.[91]

(B) American Corporate Investment in Israel

Two hundred U.S. corporations, including 23 of the Fortune 500,[92] have established manufacturing and export subsidiaries in Israel. Between

1966–1977, the total U.S. corporate investment in Israel totalled $1.6 billion, of which $108 million was in equity and intercompany account outflows. The total income of such transactions was $171 million and the corporate earnings were $163 million. Corporate reinvestment of such earnings totalled $84 million. Further, the interest, dividends and earnings of unincorporated affiliates totalled $88 million.

The value of American corporate investment in Israel gradually increased at first but, in 1972, the amount invested increased more sharply than the year before. The upward trend continued until 1975, when the amount invested increased approximately two fold. Then, in the following two years, the degree of increase was similar to the pre-1975 level. Also, the amount of intercompany outflows and equity increased sharply in 1972 and 1973, then to decline in 1974. The upward trend was restored in 1975 and 1976, then to decline in 1977. Corporate income, positive throughout the period, has ranged from $1 million in 1966 to $31 million in 1974. Notably, the period from 1972 upward marked a sharp increase in corporate income. Furthermore, corporate earnings followed the same pattern as corporate income.

American corporate income from royalties and free arrangements in Israel between 1966–1977 totalled $95 million. Exact figures on licensing arrangements are not available, but are expected to be small.

The American corporate profits and dividends that were transferred abroad amounted to $41 million in 1974, $48 million in 1975 and $50 million in 1976.[93] Around 30 percent of manufactured exports in Israel are derived from companies with foreign investment.[94]

In the period between 1966 and 1974, 68 recorded transactions of direct American corporate investment were realized. The amount of the individual investment ranged from $45,000 (made by the Near East Finance Company) to $3.1 million (made by Israel Petrochemical Enterprises Ltd.). The total American corporate investment in the above mentioned projects was $28.4 million. The industries and services established or provided included a tractor plant, electronic systems, service station construction, construction of grain silos, expansion of security facilities, etc.

Several American companies already operating in Israel were forced to cut back on their investment. For example, Monsanto Textile Co. sold 53 percent of their shares to an Israeli partner "because of the plant's small size and the fact that it does not fit their long-range plans." The company saw the need to terminate ". . . operations with inadequate profit potential."[95] Also, the case of the American Israeli Paper Mills offers an indication of the low profitability of American corporate ventures in Israel. Return on each share fluctuated and dropped from $.44 per share in 1969 to $.04 in 1975.[96] Such low profitability of foreign investment is due mainly to the small size of the Israeli market, the high cost of labor and, indirectly, to the Arab boycott of corporations that contribute to the building of Israel's war efforts. In reviewing the reports of Overseas Private Insurance Corporations and American government agencies, only four American companies insured their operations in Israel.[97] The size of investment insured totalled $9.8 million and the amount of coverage totalled $10.1 million. It seems that the majority of U.S. corporations are not deterred from investing in Israel due to fear of being nationalized. On the other hand, at the 1968 conference (mentioned earlier), an investment company was created with a working capital of $100 million for the purpose of expanding the base of Israel's industrial production. At the 1973 conference, 40 new ventures were approved, bringing the total investment to $500 million.[98]

Furthermore, several actions were taken by state governments and organizations in the U.S. to promote American corporate investment in Israel. The governors of New York, New Jersey and Connecticut signed bills permitting savings banks and credit unions to invest up to 5 percent of their assets in Israel.[99] Also, American labor unions, such as the International Ladies Garment Worker's Union, began to invest in Israeli bonds.[100]

The data on corporate investment in Israel are incomplete and often unavailable, probably because of corporate reluctance to reveal information on their business involvement in Israel out of fear that it might jeopardize existing and profitable operations in the Arab markets. But, available data do suggest the importance and significance of such investment in meeting Israel's needs and pleas for foreign exchange and for capital resources to maintain a high standard of living and to expand its industrial base. Pinhas Sapir, then Israeli Finance Minister, stated in 1973 that the $500 million investment derived from the third conference would "double Israel's GNP within the next decade."[101]

It is evident that American and foreign investment provide Israel's economy with injections to expand its industial base and uphold its ailing economy. The flow of American capital has enabled Israel to (1) achieve a high degree of capital accumulation; (2) absorb and accommodate a large number of immigrants; (3) maintain almost full employment; and (4) achieve a shift of emphasis, i.e. devote approximately 40 percent of its GNP for military expenditures without undermining governmental participation in other sectors of the economy or above all the high standard of living enjoyed by the Israelis. Furthermore, U.S. funds make it possible for Israel to preserve one of the basic tenets of Zionism which is agricultural settlements must not be eliminated or diverted into industrial projects, though some changes are already achieved in this field. Through private American assistance, Israel has been able to shift its emphasis and concentrate on military buildup, leaving health, education, immigration and many other governmental functions to be handled by the Jewish Agency, which is largely financed by donations from the U.S. and elsewhere.

Private funds plus U.S. governmental assistance are both necessary to enable Israel to meet the challenges of economic development, to purchase military equipment from abroad, and to meet the ever increasing costs of maintaining a huge armed forces to subjugate the Arab masses and to stifle Palestinian resistance in Israeli-occupied land. This enormous financial assistance has enabled Israel, for example, to erect new Israeli settlements in the occupied Arab territories in defiance of the U.S. and of world public opinion. The construction of settlements adds additional burdens on the Israeli annual budget, since the initiative costs approximately $100 million a year. Israel's continuing ability to finance new settlements has depended heavily on the flow of U.S. capital from private and governmental sources.[102]

Since 1967, Israel has taken advantage of the unlimited U.S. support and the U.S. failure to translate its verbal protests into concrete measures that might force Israel to halt the establishment of new settlements in Arab lands occupied by Israel since 1967. It is no secret that the Likud government has no intention of returning the occupied land to the Arabs; instead, it is planning to increase Jewish settlements in these territories as a step toward future annexation in order to create Greater Israel.[103] In this respect, the contributions by U.S. citizens and institutions have assisted the Israelis in carrying out their expansionist plans, thus hindering progress toward the acceptence of the Reagan plan. As long as U.S. capital continues to flow into Israel, there is no need for the Israeli government to pay much attention to the U.S. criticism of Jewish settlements in the West Bank. The U.S. must act to back up its official position on the settlement issue if it hopes to find a peaceful solution for the Arab-Israeli conflict, which has threatened U.S. economic and strategic interests in the Middle East.

3

U.S. AID TO ISRAEL: AN ASSESSMENT

Since the establishment of Israel in 1948, the U.S. has acted as a patron of the Zionist state, providing it with massive assistance to ensure its survival as a political and economic entity in the midst of the Arab world. Table 4 shows that both the U.S. government and private American sources have supplied Israel with $42.3 billion (65 billion in 1983 dollars) since 1949. These huge sums have helped Israel overcome the costs of building and maintaining a formidable military force and of meeting the challenges of sustaining a moderate rate of economic growth despite adverse conditions stemming from mounting balance-of-payment deficits and huge military expenditures. It is no secret that Israel would not have been able to meet these tasks without heavy dependence on American aid because of its meager domestic revenue sources. Israeli diplomats in Washington themselves "acknowledge their unusual vulnerability to any lessening of military, economic and financial support from abroad." They stress that "Israel's need for both military and economic aid has increased considerably since the Yom Kippur War in 1973, because any Arab arms buildup has coincided with growing Israeli foreign debt."[104] Thus, Israel has been able to overcome the costs of military buildup by relying heavily on American aid, the sale of Israeli Bonds and, to a lesser extent, loans from foreign banks.

U.S. assistance has been the mainstay of Israel's continuing ability to finance both military and development programs. U.S. administrations have supplied Israel with a total of $28.1 billion in military and economic assistance since 1949, of which $14.6 billion were given as outright grants. The U.S. has always taken into account Israel's financial needs in giving aid to the Zionist state—a situation that made Israel, a country with 3.5 million people, the largest recipient of U.S. aid.

In military assistance, the U.S. has given Israel a total of $19.1 billion from 1948 through 1984, most of which was given in the years following the 1973 War. The year 1974 marked the beginning of a sizeable increase in the amounts of U.S. military assistance to Israel and of a growing emphasis on grants. Since 1974, Israel has received a total of $25.3 billion, of which $14.2 billion are grants. These figures, including a huge amount in grants, reveal that the U.S. has subsidized Israel's military buildup, equipping it with the most sophisticated weapons in the American arsenal. With the exception of some European weapons, "almost all the equipment in the Israeli armed forces has been obtained under the U.S. government's foreign military sales program, from which Israel has received $15 billion of the $28 billion distributed worldwide from 1951 to 1982."[105] Thus, U.S. military assistance has been instrumental in helping Israel attain an unprecedented military superiority in the region.

TABLE 4
U.S. Aid to Israel, 1949–1985
(Billions of Dollars)

Source	Amount	Total in 1983 Dollars
U.S. Government Assistance (Military & Economic)	$28.1	42.3
Export–Import Bank	1.1	1.6
Private Individuals and Institutions, and Israel Bonds	14.0	21.0
Total	43.2	64.9

U.S. administrations have naively thought that Israel would simply maintain the *status quo* in the area and would use its military superiority only as a deterrent against any Arab attempt to liberate Palestine from Zionist control. The Israeli record over the past three decades has proved otherwise, however. Recent events indicate that Israel, having acquired a qualitative and technological edge over the Arab states, has increased its expansionist appetite, initiating wars not for self-defense as originally expected by the Americans but for territorial expansion, striking at will against near and far Arab targets (i.e. the Iraqi nuclear reactor, the invasion of Lebanon in 1978 and 1982) in order to maintain its military superiority and to prevent the Arabs from ever closing the military gap.

Although U.S. military assistance is intended to be used for self-defense, American policy-makers have failed to initiate stern measures to ensure that Israel does not use American military wares in offensive wars. American officials have occasionally issued mild statements protesting Israel's actions but, under no circumstances have they thought of reducing or cutting off military aid in the face of violation of U.S. law. This is primarily because the U.S. shares Israel's concerns about Arab armament and approves Israel's pre-emptive strike strategy against Arab targets in order to maintain a balance of power in favor of Israel in the region. Israel's aggressive actions have been carried out against adjacent states and any other Arab state which might be perceived as a potentially competent adversary, as in the case of Iraq. U.S. military assistance has made Israel capable of giving a "bloody nose" to Arab governments whenever confrontation is necessary to eliminate the capabilities and potential power which the Arabs might project. The rationalization is to satisfy Israeli militarism and safeguard Western interests in the highly strategic region of the Middle East.

The Israeli leaders, using the cold-war rivalry between Washington and Moscow, have convinced U.S. administrations to give them more aid and better military equipment to counter threats by the Soviet Union and by its friends in the Middle East. In response, both Democratic and Republican administrations have steadily increased the volume of U.S. military assistance even at a time when the Israeli government has been intransigent and when key Arab states have shown moderation and accommodation.

The study reveals that Israel has always taken advantage of any American initiative to move the Middle Eastern problem toward a diplomatic solution, in that the Israelis have always obtained a sizeable reward for every degree of token consent they give to the American diplomatic effort to break the stalemate in the war-torn Middle East. This was evident in the huge aid package that Israel received for accepting the Rogers initiatives and, later, Kissinger's "shuttle diplomacy." The price was even higher for Begin's acceptance of the Camp David Accords engineered by President Carter.

Between 1949–1984, the U.S. supplied Israel with $43.2 billion. (1) U.S. governmental assistance has totalled $28.1 billion, of which $14.6 billion was given as grants; (2) aid from private sources has amounted to $14 billion; (3) the Export-Import Bank has given $1.1 billion in loans; and (4) American investment is estimated to be $2 billion.

This study reveals that the U.S. has increased the volume of its economic assistance and the amounts of grants as Israel's foreign debt has worsened—a debt which reached a record high of $21.5 billion in 1983.

Recently, American aid to Israel has been questioned following Israel's invasion of Lebanon in the summer of 1982 and the subsequent slaughter of hundreds of Palestinian civilians in two refugee camps in West Beirut. As the syndicated columnist William Raspberry put it: "Those were American planes and missiles and tanks that smashed into Lebanon, leaving thousands of dead and maimed civilians, women and babies, in their wake. At some point we will have to . . . deal with the fact that weapons, supplied by us on the hard understanding that they will be used only for defensive purposes, have been used to slaughter innocents who were no threat to Israel."[106]

This questioning has come at a time when U.S.-Israel relations have been strained by the Israeli government's refusal to heed American and world appeals to halt the construction of Zionist colonies in the occupied Arab land as well as its outright rejection of Reagan's peace initiative.

Secretary of State George Shultz has been stunned by the revelation that U.S. assistance is being used to finance Israeli settlements in the West Bank, which currently cost approximately $100 million a year. U.S. funds are used to supply homes for Israeli settlers at reduced prices along with other benefits. It was reported that "new West Bank housing is supplied at less than one-half of its cost in Israel proper; the basic services and utilities are free; that some mortgage loans of up to 80 percent are not collected so long as the buyer occupies his new home."[107] It can be concluded that American aid is essential to subsidize Israel's colonization of the West Bank because the Israeli economy is overheated by its huge military expenditures and by a growing balance-of-payment deficit. Without U.S. assistance, the Israeli government would be in no position to finance the re-settlement of 100,000 Israelis in the West Bank by 1985 as a preparatory step toward annexation.

The settlement issue is a thorny one, causing strains in U.S.-Israel relations and threatening Reagan's peace initiative. American officials believe that U.S. aid, being used to construct new settlements in the occupied Arab land, has subverted Reagan's plan, which has been accepted by the Arabs and rejected by Israel. To turn Israel around, it might be necessary to consider withholding American aid until the settlements are frozen—a necessary step to lift Reagan's plan off the ground. Such a measure might be difficult to initiate because of the pro-Israel bloc in Congress, which will spare no effort to defeat the administration's move. This was evident in late December 1982 when the Senate brushed aside Reagan's plea not to increase U.S. aid to Israel in the 1983 budget over the amount suggested by the administration prior to Israel's invasion of Lebanon. The Senate action was embarrassing for the administration; it dealt a blow to its credibility with the Arab states which have hoped that the U.S. could use its leverage with Israel to move the Middle East toward a peaceful settlement. It also sent signals to the Likud leaders that they could continue to ignore Reagan's plan and still expect financial backing from the U.S. to support their absorption policy.[108] Under these circumstances, there is no hope that Reagan's initiative will succeed unless Congress is willing to support the administration's strategy to use American aid as leverage to convince the Israeli government to abandon its settlement policy in the West Bank and to agree to trade occupied Arab land for peace in the region. It is neither in the interest of the U.S. nor of Israel for the Middle Eastern conflict to continue—a conflict that has engulfed the region in an endless series of wars during the last three decades. As one observer put it: "the point is that we had better recognize—as the rest of the world already does—that we cannot supply Israel's war machine or underwrite its bellicose policies without buying into its bellicosity."[109]

The U.S. must realize that if Israel insists on illegally confiscating additional Arab territory and occupying Gaza, the West Bank, and the Golan Heights instead of seeking peace, the current cycle of attack, reprisal and expansion of Israel's "defense zones" will continue, engulfing the Middle East in more wars and undermining American strategic and economic interests in the area. It also means that U.S. taxpayers will have to carry the burden of subsidizing Israel's expansionist policy. It is doubtful whether the U.S. can continue to provide sizeable economic and military assistance to Israel at a time when Americans are suffering from deep recession and high unemployment as well as from severe budget cuts in human services in an attempt to balance the federal budget and to reduce the American government's own deficit, which runs $200 billion a year.

Part Two

4

ISRAEL IN THE 1980s
WAR OR PEACE IN THE MIDDLE EAST?

The decade of the eighties stands as a turning point in the rise of the militant, uncompromising Zionism which governs Israel today, an ideology that upholds the rights of the Jews to the West Bank, Gaza and the Golan Heights while denying the basic rights of the Palestinian people to their homeland. As Prime Minister Menachem Begin said in September 1982: "The land of our fathers and sons—Judea and Samaria (referring to the West Bank)—will be for the Jewish People for generation upon generation."[110]

The early years of this decade have already seen two crucial developments within Israel: (1) the "orientalization" of Israeli society; and (2) the consolidation of power by the Likud government. The Oriental Jews, now constituting 55 percent of the entire population, have become a decisive force in determining the outcome of the political competition between the Labor and Likud Parties. This was evident in the 1981 elections, when "65 percent of Likud's support came from Oriental Jews,"[111] and who, in the words of Austria's Chancellor at the time, Bruno Kreisky, "are full of sympathy for the semi-fascist policies of Mr. Begin and Mr. Sharon...."[112] In fact, their vote has made Begin's rule possible and has encouraged him to pursue his policies of aggression, expansion and colonization. There is little prospect that the Oriental Jews would shift their support to the Labor Party during the 1980s because of their "backwardness," as Kenneth Brown termed it, referring to "their origin in pervasively religious cultures that know only authoritarian regimes, their lack of political maturity, their emotionalism and hatred of Arabs. These attitudes and 'mentalities' are considered to have an affinity with Likud ideology and its militant, and uncompromising Zionism."[113]

Furthermore, the Likud leadership is held hostage to the memory of the holocaust, which has shaped its attitudes, strategies and policies toward its neighbors. This is exemplified in Begin's own insights into his view of Israel's attack on the Palestine Liberation Organization forces in West Beirut in the summer of 1982:

71

> I tell you . . . how I feel these days when I turn to the creator of my soul
> in deep gratitude: I feel as a prime minister empowered to instruct a
> valiant army facing "Berlin" where, amongst innocent civilians, Hitler
> and his henchmen hide in a bunker deep beneath the surface.[114]

These old memories and antagonisms blur the vision of Israel's leaders and make them incapable of seeing a need for a negotiated settlement to the Question of Palestine, which remains the crux of the Mideast conflict. On the contrary, these attitudes encourage a militant approach in a no-win situation, leaving the 4.4 million Palestinians with no alternative but to fight for their homeland.

This chapter offers an examination of the substance and direction of Israel's policies in order to shed light on what appears to be in store for the rest of this decade. This analysis will focus on (1) Israel's militarism and the Arab-Israeli conflict; (2) Israel's aggression and colonization; and (3) the prospects for peace in the Middle East and its implications for the U.S.

Israel's Militarism and the Arab-Israeli Conflict

In their efforts to establish Israel, the Zionist leaders argued that the new state would serve as a haven for Jews from all over. In their view, force is the only way to ensure the security and the survival of that country in the midst of the Arab world. This decision has caused them to emphasize military preparedness to ensure that the Israelis will never be caught off guard in a time of crisis. As a result, Israel has become a militaristic society where every adult, male and female, is trained in military warfare and must serve a tour of duty in the armed forces. Upon the completion of that tour, they automatically join reserve units and are subject to be called for active duty on short notice. In addition, Israel has created large and modern armed forces that, at present, are superior to any possible combination of regional forces. As General Mattatyahu Peled, former member of the General Staff, put it: the army can now "(f)ield a force larger than the one that fought in the Sinai without calling up the reserves."[115] Israel's active military manpower increased from 71,000 in 1967 to 174,000 in 1982—an increase of 245 percent over a 15-year period.[116]

Israeli leaders have armed the country far beyond its security needs and have developed its weapons programs as guarantees for its well-being. As General Peled put it: there are "no practical limits to Israeli defense spending."[117] Military expenditures increased from $251 million in 1962 to $2.2 billion in 1980—an increase of 884 percent in less than 20 years.[118] With U.S. assistance and technology, they have acquired the most sophisticated weapons in the American arsenal; have maintained a qualitative and technological edge over their Arab neighbors; and have developed their arms industry. In fact, Israel is the world's fourth most powerful state, preceded only by the U.S., the Soviet Union and China, and it is ranked seventh among the world's arms merchants.[119]

TABLE 5
Israel's Military Manpower and Equipment

	1967	1972	1977	1982
Active Military Manpower	71,000	77,000	164,000	174,000
Combat Aircraft	230	432	549	634
Medium Tanks	850	1,700	3,000	3,600

Source: Joe Stork and Jim Paul, "Arms Sale and the Militarization of the Middle East," *MERIP Reports,* No. 112, February 1983, pp. 7–8.

As shown in Table 5, Israel drastically increased its active military manpower and equipment between 1967 and 1982. An indirect result is that the armed forces have gained substantial voice in Israel's domestic and foreign politics. As General Peled has remarked, its substantial size "make(s) it easier for the Government to submit to the army's demands."[120] Thus, the Israelis have developed a highly complex war machinery that will be very hard to turn off or hold back in the upcoming years. This is primarily because the armed forces have played and will continue to play a major role in deciding war or peace in the Middle East. Like other strategists, the Israeli armed forces prefer a military rather than a political solution to the Arab-Israeli conflict. It is not in their interest to resolve the Palestine Question, whose continuation guarantees their influential position in the society. Israeli planners have reached the conclusion that the country's security cannot be ensured by conventional weapons alone and that nuclear weapons must be developed in preparation for future wars— wars that must be fought to secure Israel's dominance and its control of the rich mineral resources in the Middle East. Such a program is very costly and Israel, with its meager domestic resources, cannot really afford to embark on it, especially because of the already high drain that military expenditures make on the country; in all, military costs consume 40 percent of Israel's GNP. For this reason, Israel has found a natural ally in South Africa, the most racist government in the world. Israel and South Africa, both being settler states, have worked out a marriage of convenience to develop nuclear weapons that will help them subjugate the oppressed masses in their countries and in the adjacent areas. Israel has provided the technical know-how, which has been acquired from American technology and scientists, while South Africa has put up the funds for development of the nuclear weapons programs. Thus, both Israel and South Africa have pooled their resources to maintain qualitative and technological superiority over their neighbors in their joint quest for domination in two highly strategic regions of the world. The nuclear weapons programs are being developed as the ultimate weapons that will guarantee the survival of their settler regimes and the continuation of their oppression of the indigenous population. Both Israel and South Africa have refused to sign the Nuclear Non-Proliferation Treaty and have not allowed international inspection of their nuclear facilities. This situation is explosive and has already accelerated the arms race because neighboring countries cannot sit idle and permit Israel and South Africa to continue their aggression and to threaten their very existence.

Israel's militarism has led to a sharp rise in the influence of the armed forces in government circles and in the country's political decisions, which means that military solutions are likely to continue to dominate the Arab-Israeli conflict. The militarists insist that Israel's security can be guaranteed only by acquiring more Arab land rather than by pursuing a political process of negotiating a genuine peace. Consequently, Israel's military superiority has not been used as a deterrent against aggression but, instead, it has been systematically unleashed against its neighbors to cripple Arab military capabilities and to leave them vulnerable to Zionist expansion. In recent years, Israel has emerged as a powerful regional power that no longer has its back to the wall. Thus, wars are no longer "a leap into a realm of chance, desperation and improvisation," as Golda Meir once said.[121]

Israeli militarism has had a direct impact on the Arab-Israeli conflict, which will continue in the 1980s largely because Israeli leaders don't see a strong need to seek a political solution for the Palestine Question. On the contrary, they see tangible advantages in the continuation of the conflict, which has served their own objectives well. First, Israeli leaders have persistently used the Middle Eastern conflict to pressure Jews in the diaspora to respond to the "call of Aliyah"—the "ingathering" in Israel. It is a matter of life or death for Israel to increase Jewish population through immigration for three reasons: (1) to compensate for the steady decline in Jewish population resulting from Israeli citizens leaving the country to settle overseas, particularly in the U.S.; (2) to offset increases in the Arab population under Israeli jurisdiction; and (3) to use the new migrants to increase Jewish settlers in the occupied Arab territories in preparation for their incorporation into Israel, as part of a plan to create Greater Israel. Second, tension in the Middle East has rallied the Jews in the diaspora behind Israel, which is mistakenly viewed as "David fighting Goliath" to survive in a hostile region surrounded by enemies committed to its destruction. Although Israel has been the aggressor, waging wars whenever they serve its objectives, it has managed through propaganda to convince world Jewry in particular and the Western world in general that the wars are defensive rather than offensive. These wars help Israel justify taxing the Jews in the diaspora to safeguard the independence of the Zionist state and to uphold its economy, which has suffered strenuously from heavy military expenditures. As Begin put it in December 1982, following his invasion and occupation of southern Lebanon: the American Jews "will stand by our side. This is the land of their forefathers, and they have a right and duty to support it."[122]

Third, the continuation of the conflict has enabled Israel to obtain substantial military and economic assistance from the U.S. government along with generous contributions from American Jews, who have traditionally been committed to Israel's policies. The size of U.S. aid has always been shaped by the danger Israel is perceived to be facing.[123] Israeli officials have always exaggerated the Arab threat in order to attract more American governmental assistance and contributions from private citizens and organizations. U.S. assistance has, in fact, become an integral part of Israel's annual budget[124] and crucial to its herculean effort to finance its ever increasing foreign debts. For example, Israel's total foreign debt increased from $4.1 billion in 1972 to $21.5 billion in 1983.[125] These debts, in turn, result from huge costs related to the military buildup.

The Israeli economy suffers from a phenomenal rate of inflation, with the consumer price index rising over 150 percent per year. The price index increased by 24 times between 1975 and 1981 and by 21 times between January 1981 and May 1982. The Israeli trade balance has been recording deficits ranging from $3 billion to $5 billion annually (when total exports amount to about $5 billion to $6 billion). Further, Israel's budget deficit annually ranges from 20 percent to 30 percent of national expenditures. Thus, trade deficits, budget deficits and military spending absorb about 50 percent of all government spending. The combination of these factors has led to a constant erosion in the value of the Israeli shekel (from I£4.2 equal to one dollar in 1972 to 100 shekels equal to one dollar in 1983). Moreover, Israel's external debt rose by 524 percent, reaching $21.5 billion between 1972 and 1983.[126]

Clearly, the Israeli economy suffers from a score of abnormalities and serious structural deformities. In attempting to deal with the deteriorating economy, Rafael Eitan, former Israeli Chief-of-Staff, has suggested an "emergency" plan based on lower wages and no strikes.[127] The Editor-in-Chief of the *Yediot Ahronot* went even further to prescribe authoritarianism to shore up the economy and to gain economic independence:

> If we can not obtain economic independence under a democratic regime, we will have to opt for a less democratic rule, provided it is strong enough and firm enough to assure our survival, because our existence is more important than the individual freedom of each one of us.[128]

Fourth, the Israeli government has successfully used the war situation to distract attention from its domestic problems, which might otherwise disturb the precarious balance that exists between the European (Ashkenazim) "patricians" and the Oriental (Sephardim) "plebs." The gap between European and Oriental Jews is widening and is potentially very explosive. According to the 1982 Israeli Central Bureau of Statistics figures, the gross income of Oriental Jews is 40 percent lower than that of wage-earners from European background. Sami Smoucha of Haifa University indicates that only 13 percent of the Oriental Jews are employed in the elite professions, sciences and executive jobs, as opposed to 31 percent of the European Jews. The number of Oriental Jews in the Knesset and in the top positions in the civil services and public institutions is even smaller.

These domestic problems have so far been tolerated for the sake of uniting the Israelis behind the war effort against their Arab neighbors. Israeli leaders have thus avoided any serious challenge to the traditional European leadership, whether it is Likud or Labor. Moreover, Begin's brand of Zionism has distracted the Oriental Jews from demanding equality and power sharing; instead, it has rallied them behind Likud's tough policies toward the Palestinians in the occupied territories and its plan for aggression and expansion in the region.

Israeli Aggression

Invasions and wars will continue in the 1980s as long as Israel does not abandon its manipulation of various forms of coercion, including war, in the service of its political objectives. Throughout its history, Israel has demonstrated a willingness to intervene in the internal affairs of neighboring countries and to apply direct military force to achieve its own political objectives. A recent example is Israel's intervention in the Lebanese civil war in an effort to "(turn) the country into a Phalangist-controlled state,"[129] as Defense Minister Ariel Sharon, the architect of the Lebanese invasion in June 1982, envisaged.

Since 1975, Israel has allied itself with Major Saad Haddad, head of the Lebanese Christian militia, even though he has been charged with treason for forming his own militia and setting up a conclave under his command in southern Lebanon along the Israeli border. Israel has trained and armed his forces to fight the progressive Lebanese forces, who have been loosely allied with the PLO. In doing so, Israel has prolonged the Lebanese civil war and paved the ground for its own invasion of Lebanon in 1978 and again in 1982.

The Israeli government used the May 1982 attack on Israel's Ambassador in London as a pretext for conducting an all-out invasion against the PLO forces in southern Lebanon in June. The planning for this invasion had, in fact, taken place three months prior to that incident and coincided with the time when Israel was about to turn over the last portion of the Sinai to Egypt, in accordance with the Camp David Accords. Such timing reveals that Begin had no intention of living up to the commitment he made at Camp David to grant "full autonomy" to the Palestinians in the occupied territories and to halt the establishment of settlements there. It is interesting to note that Begin had secured in advance the approval of U.S. Sectetary of State Alexander Haig for the Lebanese invasion.[130] Haig shared Begin's views on what they often term "international terrorism" and the danger of a Soviet presence in the Middle East. Both Haig and Begin saw a strategic advantage in destroying the PLO strongholds in southern Lebanon in an effort to stifle radicalism in the Arab world and also to weaken Soviet influence in the area. According to a recent report, Haig gave his blessing to the Israeli invasion of Lebanon prior to his sudden resignation from the State Department. Such a revelation sheds negative light on the U.S., which has been trying to play the role of a broker in the Middle Eastern conflict.

The Israeli invasion of Lebanon in June 1982 came at a time when the PLO activities were at their lowest and with Israel's full knowledge of the British conclusion that the PLO had nothing to do with the attempt on the Ambassador's life. But the incident was all that Begin wanted to put in motion his already-drawn plan to wipe out PLO bases in neighboring Lebanon. He saw this as a necessary step in destroying the PLO once and for all so that the Palestinians would have no spokesman to defend their legitimate rights for a homeland.

Israel has, in fact, thrived on the planning of conflicts and the execution of wars since 1948. Such a strategy has kept the Middle East on the brink of war but has served Israel well. Its use of the "first strike" has guaranteed success to its military ventures. As a result, the Israelis captured and occupied Arab territories in 1956, 1967 and 1982 and used them as leverage in dealing with diplomatic initiatives seeking to ease tension in the Middle East or to resolve the Arab-Israeli conflict. This fact prompted Bertrand Russell, a renowned British philosopher, to declare:

> After every stage in this expansion Israel has appealed to "reason" and has suggested "negotiation." This is the traditional role of imperial power, because it wishes to consolidate with the least difficulty what it has already taken by violence. Every new conquest becomes the new basis of the proposed negotiations from strength, which ignores the injustice of the previous aggression.[131]

Although Israeli aggression has been continuously condemned by the United Nations, Israel has remained indifferent. This is exemplified in Begin's address to 200 American members of the United Jewish Appeal in Israel in August 1982: "Nobody should preach to us." He indicated that "Israel would continue the siege of West Beirut as it saw fit, regardless of international criticism."[132] In fact, Israeli aggression has been beneficial for the Zionist state, bringing substantial monetary gains as well as more and better American military equipment. Israel has been paid handsomely for every concession it has ever made to go along with American initiatives.

The Israelis have continuously gotten most of what they want in return for their consent to accept American initiatives. They have always prepared a long shopping list of military hardware to present to American officials as a way of seeking in advance a firm commitment on how much the U.S. is willing to pay in return for Israel's concessions. As an Israeli politician put it in August 1975, commenting on Kissinger's last minute effort to conclude a disengagement agreement in the Sinai: "Our negotiating position at this point might better be described as a shopping list."[133] *Time* magazine reported that top officials in the State Department were busy around the clock "conferring with two teams of Israeli officials, determining just what the U.S. would give in money, arms and political guarantees in exchange for Israeli concessions to Egypt."[134] This situation led Donald Neff, *Time*'s Jerusalem bureau chief, to comment: "To state it crudely, it appears that since the U.S. cannot negotiate peace in the Middle East, it will buy it."[135]

As shown below, since 1970, Israel has always received substantial military assistance for its acceptance of American initiatives:

- In 1971, following the Roger Plan, Israel received a total of $545 million in U.S. military assistance in contrast to only $30 million in the previous year.

- In 1976, following Kissinger's disengagement agreement in the Sinai, Israel received $1.5 billion in U.S. military assistance, including $850 million in grants, in contrast to $300 million in the year before.

- In 1979, following Carter's Camp David Accords, Israel received $4 billion in U.S. military assistance, including $1.3 billion in grants, in contrast to $1 billion in the previous year.

- In 1983, following Shultz's Lebanese Accord, the Reagan administration decided to release the F-16 fighter-bombers, which were originally being withheld "until the Israeli forces leave Lebanon."[136] Under this agreement, the Israelis have agreed to pull out of Lebanon only when other foreign troops—Syrian and PLO—withdraw, too.

Thus, Israel has made tremendous gains in exchange for token arrangements proposed by the U.S. to defuse tension in the Middle East and to pave the way for a dialogue that might end the Arab-Israeli conflict. These attempts, however, have failed to find a political settlement for the long drawn-out conflict because of Israel's intransigence and unreadiness to search for a political rather than military solution for the Palestine question—an issue that will determine war or peace in the Middle East in the near and distant future.

These substantial gains from aggression surely will not convince Israel to abandon its "big-stick" policies in the Middle East or to leave its neighbors alone in the 1980s. It has already established its readiness to intervene militarily in neighboring countries and to support fascist anti-PLO factions in an attempt to wipe out PLO bases along its borders. Its objective is to clear the surrounding areas of PLO forces in order to deal a blow to the Palestinian armed struggle. This can also be accomplished through intervention for the purpose of setting up puppet regimes, which are militarily weak and vulnerable to Israel's pressure. The Likud government has been using aggression to extract concessions from neighboring governments, including both the removal of PLO bases and the granting of Israel's rights to patrol or to station multinational forces on foreign soil to guarantee its security. Israel's record reveals that the use of force and coercion has worked well, enabling Israel to take advantage of Arab weakness and vulnerability to accomplish its own political objectives.

Israeli Colonization

Since 1967, both the Labor and Likud governments have made it clear that they will never agree to Israel's return to the pre-1967 borders and that Israel's security requires the acquisition of more Arab territories. Over the past few years, the Likud government specifically has made it no secret that it plans to recreate biblical Judea and Samaria—a plan which cannot be accomplished without the colonization of the West Bank and Gaza. To further this objective, the Israeli government has systematically carried out measures to uproot the Palestinians of the Galilee, West Bank, and Gaza in order to establish Greater Israel on both banks of the Jordan River.

Since 1967, Israeli policies have been designed "both to contain the size of the (Palestinian) population over whom dominance would have to be exercised and to reduce its (the Palestinian) capacity to resist domination."[137] This is done, in part, through expulsion, deportation and economic strangulation. Table 6 shows that, since the Begin government decided in 1979 to increase Jewish settlements in the West Bank, there has been increased use of selective expulsion and emigration[138] in an effort to reduce the Palestinian community to a manageable size that would make dominance and control much easier for the occupiers. Activist Palestinians have been deported; PLO sympathizers have been tortured and thrown into jail; youths have been subjected to harsh treatment and stiff fines in order to stifle national sentiment. During April 1982, for example, Israeli forces opened fire on Palestinian demonstrators, killing seven and wounding 273 persons. Israeli settlers have attacked Arab villages and towns and have carried out sabotage acts against outspoken Palestinian leaders in the occupied territories. Also, in April 1982, 15 persons were kidnapped by Jewish settlers.[139] This oppression is carried out in order to plant fear in the Palestinian community, and to encourage their exodus from the occupied territories. Recently, the Israeli military authorities put obstacles in the way of receiving funds from abroad, another measure to force these Palestinian families to leave the country.[140]

Economic strangulation has moved into full swing in recent years. Arab land and properties have been confiscated to make room for Jewish takeover and settlements. Water has also been denied to Arab farms in an effort to discourage Palestinians from farming and to get them to leave their villages to seek a livelihood elsewhere. Israeli military authorities are

withdrawn from Lebanon. To accomplish this objective, Washington has sought close coordination with Israel in Lebanon, a measure that will also improve Reagan's standing in the American Jewish community, whose support will enhance his chances of an electoral victory in the November election.[194]

There are serious implications to this recent shift toward U.S.-Israeli cooperation. It certainly does not guarantee that the U.S. Marines will be coming home soon as it is doubtful that they can mount enough pressure to persuade Syria's President Hafez Assad to pull his troops out of Lebanon. This conclusion is reached by the Pentagon strategists, who, "noting the speed with which the Soviet Union rearmed Syria (in 1982), doubt whether U.S.-Israeli military posturing will impress either the Syrians or the Soviets."[195] In fact, Assad is now in a strong bargaining position: First, Syria has been receiving new, sophisticated weapons from Moscow in order to enable it to withstand American-Israeli military pressure and to replace equipment destroyed during their attacks. Second, Syria has consolidated its grip on northern Lebanon by helping the rebel factions of the PLO to oust Arafat and his loyalist troops from Tripoli. Third, by supporting factions opposed to the Gemayel government, "Syria has become the key player in that fractured country's future."[196] The net result is that there is little that the U.S. can do to get a settlement out of the Syrians unless the Reagan administration is willing to get more involved in the Lebanese civil war, which already has all the ingredients of a Vietnam-type conflict. This is certainly an undesirable prospect for Reagan in an election year.

It appears that the U.S. is following Israeli advice to initiate a series of "disincentives" to pressure Syria out of Lebanon: (1) On the eve of Shamir's visit, Reagan decided to keep the battleship USS New Jersey off the Lebanese coast indefinitely; (2) The U.S. carried out a belated retaliatory raid on Syrian positions in Lebanon on December 4, 1983, coming in the aftermath of a similar Israeli attack; (3) Shortly thereafter, it was decided to establish a policy of instant retaliation in an effort to protect the U.S. Marines in Beirut and to discourage attacks on American targets in the Middle East.

The use of such "gunboat diplomacy" is a dangerous course that is likely to get the U.S. directly involved in a war that will not serve its vital interests in the Middle East. In response to the U.S. actions, Syrian officials have denounced U.S. attacks on their positions in Lebanon and have made it clear that their government would not "budge an inch" from its stance on Lebanon despite the mounting American pressure.[197] This situation is likely to lead to a major war with a possibility of "forc(ing) both the U.S.

and the Soviet Union to become more deeply and dangerously entwined in
the Middle East than perhaps either superpower would like."[198]
    There is evidence already that the area of conflict will be widened. An
example is the suicide bomb attack on the U.S. Embassy in Kuwait on
December 12, 1983. This incident might signal the beginning of a campaign
against American interests in the Middle East and, possibly, against targets
inside the U.S. There is little the U.S. can do to prevent such attacks.
However, the U.S. can end such attacks if it distances itself from Israel and
becomes neutral in the Lebanese civil war. Thus, the present policy of
cooperation with Israel does not appear to be likely to bring the Marines
home before the presidential election campaign is underway. The prospects
would be different if the Israelis were willing to deploy their military north
of the Awali River, but Israel has no interest in getting more deeply
involved in the Lebanese civil war. In fact, morale is presently low in Israel
because of the heavy casualties inflicted on Israeli troops by the Lebanese/
Palestinian Resistance Movement in southern Lebanon. Consequently,
Shamir is under pressure to end Israel's involvement in Lebanon as soon as
possible, "The Israelis seem little interested in doing anything in Lebanon
these days except cutting their losses on a timetable of their own choosing.
But this stage of the mess is Israel's doing, and Israel has a responsibility to
help American diplomacy clean it up."[199]
    By making Israel into the pre-eminent American ally in the Middle
East, Reagan has ended his efforts to play an evenhanded, mediator's role
in the region. The immediate result is a shelving of his own peace plan
(1982), which aimed at finding a permanent solution to the long-drawn-out
Arab-Israeli conflict. Thus, Israeli aggression has paid off well for Israel,
since the U.S. has shifted its focus away from finding a broader settlement
to the Palestinian problem and is now dealing only with the fallout from
Israel's invasion of Lebanon.
    Another significant result is that the U.S. is now at arm's length with
its traditional Arab allies, who have looked to the U.S. to find ways to
defuse the explosive situation in the Middle East. Reagan has undermined
his ability to act as a broker in the search for a permanent solution to the
Middle East conflict. Egypt's President Housni Mubarak has called the
U.S.-Israeli military cooperation pact "an obstacle" to the peace process
and has expressed dismay that the U.S. is openly "taking sides" when it is
supposed to act as a "judge" between the Israelis and the Arabs.[200] Similar
criticism has been voiced by other leaders, including Saudi Arabia's King
Fahd and Jordan's King Hussein. Hussein felt that the expanded strategic

ties with Israel will be accomplished at the expense of U.S.'s Arab allies. He criticized the Reagan administration for concluding the strategic cooperation agreement "without winning Israeli concessions" on broader regional issues and noted that this action is likely to undermine U.S. credibility throughout the Arab World. In Hussein's view, the agreement is a "reward" to Israel despite "(its) rejection of Reagan's peace initiative last year, its defiance of the president's call for a freeze on Jewish settlements in the occupied West Bank, and its continued occupation of southern Lebanon."[201] Prince Bandar Bin Sultan, the Saudi Arabian Ambassador to the U.S., commented that "Israel is a strategic liability to America, and their behavior in the past has not been improved by goodwill gestures from this country. . . . The past history of Israeli actions is that they ask for something and don't give anything in return."[202]

At this juncture, the Reagan administration needs to reassess its new policy toward the Middle East based on close strategic cooperation with Israel. Israeli comments following the conclusion of the recent agreement underscore this need. On November 30, Israel's Defense Minister Moshe Arens said in Washington that "the Shamir government does not intend to abandon policies that had helped to create the earlier U.S.-Israeli tensions." Shamir remains strongly opposed to the Reagan peace proposal that would grant the West Bank and Gaza independence in association with Jordan. He and Arens insist on making these Arab territories permanent parts of Israel, regardless of their huge Palestinian populations. As Arens put it, "Israel has been there for 16 years. . . . I guess if you look again in another 16 years, we will still be there."[203] In addition, the Shamir government has shown no sign of flexibility on its opposition to U.S. arms sales to moderate Arab regimes such as Saudi Arabia and Jordan.

The U.S. would be well-advised to look after its own interests in the Middle East which are, obviously, in conflict with the Zionist plans for establishing Greater Israel. In dealing with the Lebanese crisis, American officials should review the facts in order to conclude the ambiguous U.S. mission in Lebanon and to bring the U.S. Marines home. First, it was Israel's invasion of Lebanon in June 1982, that brought about the deployment of the U.S. Marines in Beirut as part of the multinational peacekeeping force. Then, in October 1983, Israel's unilateral decision to withdraw from the Chouf Mountains near Beirut exposed the flanks of the Marines at the Beirut airport, leaving them dangerously vulnerable to attack by Lebanese feuding factions. Second, it was Israel that has kept the civil war brewing in Lebanon by providing aid to conflicting factions and by refusing to withdraw from southern Lebanon until all foreign forces withdraw too. It should be noted that the agreement sponsored by the U.S. on May 17, 1983 was signed by Israel and the Phalange dominated Lebanon. Syria was not party to that agreement, a situation that will make it unlikely for Syria to comply with it, since it will lead to Lebanon's recognition of Israel. Third, it is Israel, not Syria, that continues to occupy Lebanon, since Syria's presence is legitimized by the mandate given Syria by the Arab League to separate the feuding factions as a way to prevent further deterioration in the civil war.

As long as Israel, backed by the U.S., insists on the implementation of the May agreement, the stalemate will continue in Lebanon. This means that the U.S. will increasingly find itself trapped in Lebanon with its Marines vulnerable to attack at the Beirut airport. There is a need to find a way to end the deadlock in Lebanon, but siding with Israel is definitely not the solution and is likely to complicate U.S. presence in the Middle East. The U.S. cannot afford to ignore the Palestinian problem which is the crux of the Arab-Israeli conflict. This problem cannot be solved by close cooperation with an Israeli government that has committed itself to spending $30 billion in ten years (almost ten times as much as the total U.S. aid package each year) to colonize the West Bank by erecting new Jewish settlements and by encouraging Jewish immigrants to settle there.[204] The growing Jewish settlement in the occupied Arab land will make it extremely difficult to find a just solution to the plight of the uprooted Palestinians. The U.S. cannot turn the other cheek on Israel's spending billions and billions of dollars on constructing new Jewish settlements in the occupied territories, while Israel continues to ask the U.S. to increase its overall aid levels to deal with her growing foreign debt burden. Israel, with its meager domestic resources, cannot finance its colonization program without annual American subsidies, especially in the light of the fact that Israel is now going through its worst economic crisis. Also, it is unfair for American taxpayers to finance Israel's expansion at a time when there is a great deal of suffering in the U.S. from drastic cuts made in domestic programs in order to balance the federal budget and to control its growing deficit.

Conclusion

The coming of Shamir has brought about a low key style to the Israeli government and helped pave the way for ending the frosty U.S.-Israeli relationship of the past three years. In November 1983, the first visit by Prime Minister Shamir produced startling results, ushering a new era of close, formal cooperation between the two countries.

In assessing the new partnership, it is clear that Israel, not the U.S., is the main beneficiary. The Israelis have finally established a formal alliance with the U.S., something that they have sought for decades. Israel now has U.S. backing and pledges of increased American aid to help it maintain its military superiority in the Middle East. Israel has also been assured that the U.S. will not agree to any revision in the Israeli-Lebanese agreement of May 1983, a revision that is necessary to induce Syria to withdraw from Lebanon and that might help the Gemayel government to achieve national reconciliation in the war-torn country. The implementation of the agreement is important for Israel since it will ultimately lead to Lebanon's recognition of the Zionist state, making it the second Arab state to render such a recognition. It seems that the Reagan administration is promoting Israel's interest in the Arab World and insisting that Israel must be rewarded for its invasion and occupation of Lebanon. Under these circumstances, there is no need for Israel to change its policy of coercion, including the use of force, since it has always paid off well. This situation will not restore peace and tranquility to the Middle East; instead, it will add more fuel to the fire, leading to the eruption of more wars.

It is doubtful that close strategic cooperation with Israel will help the U.S. extricate the Marines from Beirut before the 1984 presidential election campaign is under way. There is little the U.S. can do to Syria, which has consolidated its grip over northern Lebanon and has become a key player in any settlement for the Lebanese crisis. The U.S. has in fact undermined its mediator role in Lebanon by its strategic cooperation pact with Israel. It has undercut the Saudi diplomatic efforts to persuade Syria's President Hafez Assad to withdraw his troops from Lebanon. It has also made it difficult for the Gemayel government's efforts for national reconciliation, since Syrian-backed factions have demanded some revisions in the Israeli-Lebanese agreement as a first step toward solving the Lebanese crisis and getting all foreign troops out of Lebanon.

The Reagan administration is short-sighted in concluding the strategic cooperation agreement with Israel, which is likely to harm vital U.S. interests in the Arab World. *First,* it is undermining U.S. credibility in the region, since its tilt toward Israel will put the U.S. at arm's length with moderate Arab states, the traditional allies for the U.S. in the Arab World. *Second,* it marks an end to an evenhanded approach to the Middle Eastern conflict, thus terminating the peace process that had started with President Carter's Camp David Accords. This is particularly true because Reagan and Shamir strongly disagree on the Reagan peace plan of 1982, which is quietly being put to rest. *Third,* Israel is in no position to protect American interests or to check Soviet influence in the Middle East. It is the Arab states, not Israel, that hold the key to spreading or halting Soviet influence in the region. In addition, Soviet influence in the Middle East is at a low point, being limited mainly to Syria among the front-line states. In fact, the U.S.-Israeli agreement might indirectly help the spread of Soviet influence beyond Syria by allowing the Soviets to demonstrate their true friendship toward the Arabs. Under these circumstances, it will be difficult for Israel to check Soviet advances unless it is willing to unleash its army, with the U.S. backing, against progressive forces in the region. *Fourth,* while it is true that cooperation with Israel might improve Reagan's standing in the American Jewish community, it might also discourage Democrats from turning the continued presence of the U.S. Marines in Lebanon into a major campaign issue in 1984. The Democratic Party, a traditional ally for Israel, may find it extremely difficult to alienate the influential Jewish community by turning its back on Israel now. Thus, election politics might have convinced the Republican leaders to conclude the strategic cooperation agreement as a way to pull the rug from underneath the Democrats. It should be noted that the Democratic Congress has backed Reagan's decision to extend the stay of the Marines in Beirut until April 1985.

The U.S. is paying a high price and taking a great deal of risk in return for Israel's friendship. The U.S. has already given Israel more than $2 billion a year, which, if Reagan gets his way, will be all given as a gift (as outright grants rather than partially as loans). Most American aid is spent on military buildup and weapon development programs. Israel will receive $1.7 billion in military assistance compared to only $910 million in economic assistance for the next fiscal year. This is a lopsided aid program, particularly since Israel is going through the worst economic crisis in its history. It is inconceivable that the U.S. will provide Israel with funds to increase its military capability far beyond its security needs, since it is generally acknowledged that Israel is the major military power in the Middle East and is capable of striking at will anywhere in the region.

Some Americans are beginning to question the size and nature of U.S. aid to Israel because there seems to be no limit to Israel's expectations from the U.S. During his visit in November, Shamir asked for an increase in the overall aid levels in both categories from the Reagan administration, which is receptive to Israel's appeals, particularly in an election year. It is reported that Reagan has promised an increase in U.S. assistance to Israel in 1986. The increase in U.S. aid will not help the cause of peace nor further

American interests in the highly strategic region of the Middle East. On the contrary, it might encourage Israel to be bolder in its expansionist policy, which might lead to a bigger and bloodier war with a possibility of dragging the U.S. into a military confrontation with the Soviet Union.

American policy-makers would be wise to find ways to reduce U.S. aid to Israel. If the peace process that began with Carter would continue to its ultimate conclusion, the U.S. would be saving billions of dollars in military assistance. This of course will depend on whether any administration is willing to pressure Israel to find a just and lasting solution to the Palestinian problem. There is no way that peace can be found without checking Israel's expansionism. Its colonization of Arab territories will prolong the conflict and get the U.S. directly involved in the Arab-Israeli conflict simply because the U.S. is now a formal ally of Israel. Failure to solve the Palestinian problem will mean that the U.S. will continue pouring billions of dollars into Israel's war machinery. It is doubtful that the U.S. can continue the spiraling increase in U.S. assistance very long, considering the state of the American economy, with its growing federal deficit and drastic cuts in domestic programs.

The U.S. needs to take a hard look at U.S. assistance to Israel because the GAO has concluded that Israel will request more aid from the U.S. just to ease the debt service burden. Israel will not only ask for better terms, which will mean more aid given as outright grants rather than loans, but also will seek an increase in the overall level of assistance. Under these circumstances, American policy-makers will "be confronted more directly than in the past with some difficult questions concerning the U.S.-Israeli relationship. How much aid to Israel is enough? What are the risks involved in continuing the upward spiral in the aid level? And particularly with a new government taking over in Israel, what should the United States expect in return for its assistance?"[205]

NOTES

Foreword

1. *The New York Times,* November 30, 1983, p. 6.

2. *Report of the Comptroller General of the United States,* "U.S. Assistance to Israel," General Accounting Office, United States, June 24, 1983, Document Handling and Information Services Facility, P.O. Box 6015, Gaithersburg, Maryland 20760.

3. Hereinafter cited simply as "uncensored version." Copies may be obtained from the ADC, 1731 Connecticut Ave., N.W., Washington, D.C. 20009.

4. *Journal of Palestine Studies,* Institute for Palestine Studies and Kuwait University, P.O. Box 19449, Washington, D.C. 20036, Vol. XIII, No. 3, Fall, 1983, p. 124.

5. "Uncensored Version," p. 12.

6. *Ibid.,* p. 52.

7. *Ibid.,* p. 58.

8. *Ibid.,* p. 59.

9. *Ibid.,* p. 58.

10. *Op. cit., Journal of Palestine Studies,* p. 124.

11. See Ian Lustick, *Arabs in the Jewish State,* University of Texas Press, Austin, Texas, 1980.

12. See Elmer Berger, *A Critique of the Department of State's 1981 Country Report on Human Rights in Israel,* Americans for Middle East Understanding, 475 Riverside Drive, N.Y. 10115.

13. *The Longest War: Israel in Lebanon,* Alfred A. Knopf, N.Y., 1982, p. 25.

14. See Michael Sterner, "The Arabs' Next Move," *The New York Times,* January 19, 1983, p. 25.

15. Mattatyahu Peled, "Too Much Rope," *The New York Times,* December 30, 1982, p. 21.

16. "Israel's Global Ambitions," *The New York Times,* January 6, 1983, p. 31.

17. Isaiah, 58:6.

18. Jonathan Spivak, "Built By Immigration, Israel Now Is Worried About Steady Outflow," *The Wall Street Journal,* January 17, 1983, pp. 1, 17.

19. *Op. cit., The Longest War: Israel in Lebanon,* p. 115.

20. *Ibid.,* p. 114.

21. *Op. cit., Journal of Palestine Studies,* p. 124.

22. *The Wall Street Journal,* October 7, 1983, p. 36.

Introduction

1. Chaim Weizmann, *Trial and Error: The Autobiography of Chaim Weizmann.* New York: Schocken Books, 1966, p. 165.

106   American Aid to Israel

2. Sydney N. Fisher, *The Middle East: A History*. New York: Alfred A. Knopf, 1969, p. 371.

3. George Antonius, *The Arab Awakening*. New York: Capricorn Books, 1965, pp. 164-183.

4. Alfred M. Lilienthal, *What Price Israel?* Chicago: Henry Regnery Co., 1953, p. 26.

5. Fisher, pp. 427, 431.

6. J. C. Hurewitz, *Diplomacy in the Near and Middle East*. Princeton: D. Van Nostrand Co., 1956, Vol. II, pp. 218-226.

7. J. C. Hurewitz, *The Struggle for Palestine*. New York: W. W. Norton & Co., 1950, p. 143.

8. Richard P. Stevens, *American Zionism and U.S. Foreign Policy (1942-1947)*. New York: Pageant Press, 1962, p. 25; Zionist Organization of America, *Report of Activities, 1940-1946*, pp. 4-5.

9. Morris Ernst, *So Far So Good*. New York: Harper and Brothers, 1948, pp. 172-175.

10. Harry S Truman, *Memoirs*. New York: Doubleday & Co., 1956, Vol. II, pp. 133-134.

11. Harry S Truman, *Memoirs*. New York: Doubleday & Co., 1955, Vol. I, pp. 68-69; James Forrestal, *Forrestal Diaries*. New York: The Viking Press, 1951, pp. 347-348.

12. President Truman told American Ambassadors to Arab states, who had come to inform him of the deteriorating U.S. position in the Middle East: "I'm sorry, gentlemen, but I have to answer to hundreds of thousands who are anxious for the success of Zionism; I do not have hundreds of thousands of Arabs among my constituents." William A. Eddy, *FDR Meets Ibn Saud*. New York: American Friends of the Middle East, 1954, p. 37.

On November 6, 1947, Senator McGrath, the Democratic National Chairman, told Secretary of Defense James Forrestal that "there were two or three pivotal states which could not be carried without the support of people who were deeply interested in the Palestine Question." Forrestal, p. 344.

13. Truman, Vol. II, p. 164.

14. Senator Connally (D-Texas), Chairman of the Senate Foreign Relations Committee, commented in late 1945 that "Democratic members of Congress from such states as New York, Connecticut, Pennsylvania, Illinois and California (looked) to their virtually unanimous support of the (pro-Zionist) resolution to boost their chances of reelection next year." *Congressional Record*, Vol. 91, Part 9, 79th Congress, 1st Session, p. 12389.

On October 9, 1947, President Truman instructed the State Department to support the partition of Palestine in the United Nations only three days after Postmaster General Hannigan told him that "many people who had contributed to the Democratic campaign fund in 1944 were pressing hard for assurances from the administration of definitive support for the Jewish position in Palestine." Forrestal, p. 323; Truman, Vol. II, p. 155.

15. *U.S. Department of State Bulletin*, July 1982, p. 75.

16. *Ibid.*

17. *Ibid.*, April 1982, p. 83.

18. *Time*, August 16, 1982, p. 13.

19. *The Washington Post*, December 19, 1982.

20. *Ibid.*, October 1, 1982.

21. *Ibid.*, December 19, 1982.

22. *Ibid.*, November 10, 1982.

23. *Ibid.*, January 4, 1983.

24. *U.S. Department of State Bulletin,* July 1982, p. 74.

25. "It is not that we have no control over Israel," a former Pentagon official said in July, 1982. "It's that we have chosen not to exercise that control." "Officials said privately that U.S. unwillingness to use the full weight of its influence to clamp down on Israel is traceable to politics, strategy and the web of interlocking industrial, economic and military interests that bind the two countries." *The Washington Post,* July 21, 1982.

Chapter 1

26. Samir A. Rabbo, "American Aid to Israel: 'A Patron-Client' Relationship," *The Search,* Vol. 1, No. 1, Winter 1980, p. 25.

27. Martin C. McGuire, "U.S. Assistance, Israeli Allocation, and the Arms Race in the Middle East: An Analysis of Three Independent Resource Allocation Process," *The Journal of Conflict Resolution,* Vol. 26, No 2, June 1982, p. 201.

28. *Ibid.*, p. 220.

29. *Ibid.*

30. *U.S. Department of State Bulletin,* July 1982, p. 75.

31. *Ibid.*

32. *Time,* August 25, 1975, p. 24.

33. *Ibid.*

34. *The Washington Post,* July 21, 1982.

35. *DISAM Newsletter,* Vol. 4, No. 3, Spring 1982, p. 12.

36. *U.S. Department of State Bulletin,* February 22, 1954, p. 274.

37. *Ibid.*, February 9, 1953, p. 214.

38. Public Law 87-195, Part II, Sec. 501.

39. *Time,* August 10, 1970, p. 21.

40. *Ibid;* Robert Stephens, *Nasser: A Political Biography.* New York: Simon and Schuster, 1971, p. 545.

41. *Time,* August 10, 1970, p. 14.

42. Alfred M. Lilienthal, *The Zionist Connection: What Price Peace?* New York: Middle East Perspective, Inc., 1978, 1979, p. 764.

43. *Time,* March 22, 1976, p. 23.

44. McGuire, p. 221.

45. *Ibid.*, p. 223.

46. U.S. Department of State, *The Camp David Summit, September 1978.* Department of State Publication 8954, September 1978, pp. 6-9.

47. Ben Netanyahu, Deputy Chief of mission at the Israeli Embassy in Washington,

D.C., "Israel Needs the West Bank," *The Washington Post,* December 28, 1982; *Time,* August 10, 1970, p. 23; *Time,* January 11, 1982, p. 33.

48. *The Washington Post,* January 15, 1982.

49. *The Sunday Times,* June 19, 1977.

50. Secretary of State Alexander M. Haig, Jr., "NATO and Restoring U.S. Leadership." U.S. Department of State, Bureau of Public Affairs, Washington, D.C., May 9, 1981, p. 2.

51. *The Washington Post,* December 19, 1981.

52. *U.S. News & World Report,* January 11, 1982, p. 33.

53. *The Washington Post,* December 19, 1981,

54. *The Washington Post,* October 1, 1982.

55. *The Washington Post,* December 19, 1982.

56. Herman Fr. Eilts, "President Reagan's Middle East Peace Initiative," *American-Arab Affairs,* No. 2, Fall 1982, p. 1.

57. *Time,* September 20, 1982, p. 24.

58. *The Washington Post,* December 4, 1982.

59. *The Washington Post,* December 18, 1982.

60. *The Washington Report on Middle East Affairs,* Vol. 2, No. 4, p. 3.

Chapter 2

61. U.S. Agency for International Development, Report on the Israeli Economy and Debt Repayment Prospects, March 1982, pp. 2, 4, 12.

62. *Ibid.,* p. 1.

63. *Ibid.*

64. *Ibid.*

65. *The Mideast Observer in Washington,* June 1, 1981, p. 2.

66. *U.S. Department of State Bulletin,* February 8, 1954, p. 210.

67. *The Washington Post,* December 1, 1982.

68. *The Washington Post,* December 3, 1982.

69. *Ibid.*

70. U.S. Agency for International Development, Report on the Israeli Economy and Debt Repayment Prospects, January 1980, Table 1.

71. *The Washington Post,* November 10, 1982.

72. Lilienthal, *Zionist,* p. 763.

73. *Ibid.*

74. *Ibid.*

75. *Encyclopedia Judaica,* No. 10, p. 913–914.

76. Elmer Berger, *An Anlaysis of the Zionist Jewish Agency Structure.* New York: American Council for Judaism, 1963, p. 34.

77. *The Economists,* May 17, 1975, p. 72.

78. *Encyclopedia Judaica,* No. 9, pp. 539–540.

79. *The New York Times,* February 28, 1972.

80. Lilienthal, *Zionist,* p. 761.

81. Amnon E. Rafael, "The Problems of American Investment in Israel," *Israel Law Review,* Vol. 6, No. 6, 1971, 534–546.

82. Amnon E. Rafael, "Tax Reform in Israel," *Israel Law Review,* Vol. II. No. 2, 1976, p. 187.

83. *Ibid.*

84. "Africa and the Middle East," *IL & T,* September 1978, p. 3.

85. Lilienthal, *Zionist,* p. 276.

86. AID, *Report,* January 1980, p. 1.

87. *The New York Times,* August 10, 1967.

88. *The Economist,* April 13, 1968, p. 68.

89. *The New York Times,* May 10, 1973.

90. *U.S. Treaties and Other International Agreements,* Vol. 28, Part 5, 1976–1977. Washington, D.C., Department of State, pp. 3186 and 5816.

91. *Ibid.*

92. *IL & T,* September 1978, p. 4.

93. *Ibid.*

94. *Ibid.*

95. *The Wall Street Journal,* December 5, 1977.

96. *The Wall Street Journal,* January 30, 1970 and February 15, 1977.

97. *OPIC Annual Report,* 1976, pp. 44–53.

98. *The New York Times,* June 2, 1973.

99. *The New York Times,* February 28, 1972.

100. *The New York Times,* June 9, 1967.

101. *The New York Times,* June 2, 1973.

102. *The Washington Post,* November 10, 1982.

103. *U.S. News & World Report,* January 11, 1982, p. 33; *The Washington Post,* December 28, 1982 and January 4, 1983.

Chapter 3

104. *The Washington Post,* July 21, 1982.

105. *Ibid.*

106. *The Washington Post,* June 28, 1982.

107. *The Washington Post,* November 10, 1982.

108. *The Washington Post,* December 18, 1982.

109. *The Washington Post,* June 28, 1982.

Chapter 4

110. *Time,* September 20, 1982, p. 24.

111. Kenneth Brown, "Iron and a King: The Likud and Oriental Jews," *MERIP Reports,* No. 114, May 1983, p. 4.

112. *Ibid.,* p. 3.

113. *Ibid.,* p. 4.

114. *Newsweek,* August 16, 1982, p. 10.

115. *The New York Times,* December 30, 1982.

116. Joe Stork and Jim Paul, "Arms Sale and the Militarization of the Middle East," *MERIP Reports,* No. 112, February 1983, p. 7.

117. *The New York Times,* December 30, 1982.

118. Stork, p. 9.

119. *Time,* September 20, 1982, p. 25.

120. *The New York Times,* December 30, 1982.

121. *Newsweek,* August 16, 1982, p. 5.

122. *The New York Times,* December 21, 1982.

123. McGuire, p. 217.

124. *Ibid.,* p. 220.

125. AID, Report, January 1980, Table 3.

126. *Ibid.*

127. *The Jerusalem Post* (International Edition), December 30, 1979–January 5, 1980.

128. *The Yediot Ahronot,* September 14, 1979.

129. *Time,* June 28, 1982, p. 11.

130. *The Washington Post,* June 5, 1983.

131. *Middle East International* (London), No. 192, January 21, 1983, p. 19.

132. *The New York Times,* August 5, 1982.

133. *Time,* August 25, 1975, p. 24.

134. *Ibid.,* p. 18.

135. *Ibid.*

136. *The Washington Post,* April 2, 1983.

137. Janet L. Abu-Lughod, "Demographic Consequences of the Occupation," *MERIP Reports,* No. 115, June 1983, p. 14.

138. *Ibid.,* p. 16.

139. Attallah Najar, "Goodman Was Not Alone," *I & P,* May–June 1982, p. 10.

140. Abu-Lughod, p. 15.

141. *Ibid.,* p. 17.

142. *Ibid.,* p. 14.

143. *The Washington Post,* April 7, 1983.

144. *Ibid.*

145. U.N. Special Unit on Palestinian Rights, *Bulletin* Nos. 9–10, September–October 1979.

146. *The Jerusalem Post* (International Edition), December 30, 1979–January 5, 1980.

147. For more information on Eitan's position, see: Donald S. Will, "Zionist Settlement Ideology and Its Ramifications for the Palestinian People." *JPS*, Vol. XI, No. 3, pp. 47–50.

148. Quoted in Israel Shahak, tr. & ed., *The Zionist Plan for the Middle East.* Special Document No. 1, Belmont: AAUG, Inc., 1982, p. 10.

149. Abu-Lughod, p. 17.

150. "A Strategy for Israel in the Nineteen Eighties," *Kuvunim* (Directions), No. 14, Winter 1982, 5742.

151. *The Washington Post,* January 18, 1983.

152. *Ibid.*

153. *Time,* September 20, 1982, p. 24.

154. *The Washington Post,* April 11, 1983.

155. *Time,* April 12, 1982, p. 25.

156. *The Washington Post,* January 15, 1983.

157. *The New York Times,* August 9, 1982.

158. *The Washington Post,* January 15, 1983.

159. *Ibid.*

160. *The Washington Post,* February 2, 1983.

161. *The Washington Post,* April 7, 1983.

162. *Time,* April 12, 1982, p. 25.

163. *Time,* October 4, 1982, p. 26.

164. *Newsweek,* April 16, 1982, p. 15.

165. *Time,* October 4, 1982, p. 26.

166. *Time,* April 12, 1982, p. 25.

167. *The Washington Post,* June 25, 1983.

168. *Davar,* December 17, 1982.

169. Israel Shahak, *op. cit.,* p. 11.

Chapter 5

170. *Newsweek,* September 12, 1983, p. 45.

171. *Ibid.*

172. *Time,* September 12, 1983, p. 34.

173. Edward Walsh, "Begin's Unpaid Bills: Will We Help Clean Up Israel's Economic Mess?", *The Washington Post,* September 4, 1983.

174. *Ibid.*

175. *Ibid.*

176. *Ibid.*

177. The Uncensored Report of the U.S. General Accounting Office, *U.S. Assistance to the State of Israel*, June 24, 1983, p. 12.

178. Walsh.

179. *Ibid.*

180. Philip Geyelin, "Cloud Over Israel," *Ibid.*, November 29, 1983.

181. *The New York Times*, November 30, 1983.

182. *Time*, December 12, 1983, p. 19; *The Washington Post*, November 30, 1983.

183. *Ibid.*

184. *Time*, December 12, 1983.

185. *The Washington Post*, November 27, 1983.

186. *The Washington Post*, November 29, 1983.

187. *The Washington Post*, November 27, 1983.

188. *Time*, December 12, 1983, p. 19.

189. *The Washington Post*, November 30, 1983.

190. *The Washington Post*, December 4, 1983.

191. *The New York Times*, December 24, 1983.

192. Jack Anderson, "U.S.-Israeli Strategy Fought by Pentagon," *The Washington Post*, December 20, 1983.

193. *The Washington Post*, November 28, 1983.

194. *Time*, December 12, 1983, pp. 19–20.

195. Anderson, *The Washington Post*, December 20, 1983.

196. *Time*, December 19, 1983, p. 26.

197. *The Washington Post*, December 17, 1983.

198. *Time*, December 19, 1983, p. 26.

199. *The Washington Post*, November 29, 1983.

200. *The Washington Post*, December 4, 1983.

201. *The Washington Post*, December 2, 1983.

202. *The Washington Post*, December 4, 1983.

203. *The Washington Post*, December 1, 1983.

204. *The Washington Post*, November 29, 1983.

205. *The Washington Post*, September 4, 1983.

Part Three

A censored version of the GAO report on U.S. assistance to Israel was released by the General Accounting Office on June 24, 1983, almost three months after it was completed and circulated throughout the government. Below are sample pages of the censored version.

<u>Foreign policy considerations</u>

    Many consider FMS assistance as a policy statement of U.S. support for Israel.

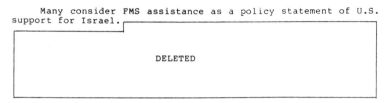

DELETED

    We were told that decisions regarding FMS are made at the highest levels of the administration.

DELETED

                       The assistance levels are determined by policy considerations beyond those involving only basic defense needs.

<u>FMS to Israel linked with Egypt</u>

    The Egyptian and Israeli FMS assistance programs are polit- ically tied to each other and are becoming more difficult to separate. The Egyptians have been requesting treatment similar to the Israelis since Camp David. This is reflected in higher levels of assistance, similar terms of FMS repayment, similar uses of cash flow (see p. 20), and similar desires for advanced equipment.

DELETE

<u>ISRAELI MILITARY NEEDS</u>

    U.S. and Israeli officials agree that Israel has security problems which require FMS assistance. However, there is grow- ing concern in Israel over the level of FMS due to: increasing U.S. arms sales to Arab countries; erosion of its qualitative advantage; and Israeli force modernization needs.

DELETED

<u>Effect of other U.S. Middle East</u>
<u>arms sales and assistance</u>

    U.S. arms sales and FMS assistance to Israel are not only linked to Egypt but also to certain other Arab countries which have or can get the funds to pay for these arms. Arms sales to an Arab State in the region generally have led to another sale to Israel or increased FMS to offset Israeli security concerns. This, Soviet sales, and the floor effect have resulted in a spiral of arms sales to the region and assistance levels.

Current controversy in arms sales to the Arabs began with
the sale of F-15 aircraft to Saudi Arabia in 1978. When the
administration presented its case for the sale, it said this was
not a single sale but a package of aircraft sales to three
Middle East countries, with 15 F-15 and 75 F-16 aircraft going
to Israel, 60 F-15 aircraft to Saudi Arabia, and 50 F-5E
aircraft to Egypt.

The Carter administration said the package approach
enhanced U.S. interests in the region and those of all three
recipient countries. It also helped ensure the security of
Israel, which opposed the sale of the F-15 aircraft to the
Saudis, by helping to maintain the balance of Arab and Israeli
air forces in the Middle East region. The administration linked
the sales to the three countries so that it was more difficult
for the Congress to isolate action on the Saudi F-15 aircraft
sale from action on the aircraft sales to Egypt and Israel.

DELETED

DELETED

Israel takes a pessimistic view of the trend of U.S. arms
sales to Arab countries and fears that the focus of U.S.
regional concern is shifting toward the Persian Gulf and Saudi
Arabia.

DELETED

Israeli concerns for threat from the region

Israelis are particularly sensitive to the level of casualties they might sustain in a full-scale war with the Arabs.

DELETED

11

Since the release of the censored version, an uncensored version of the
draft report has been obtained. Most of the information that was deleted
is included. The previously deleted information is distinguished by **bold
face type.**

Draft of a Proposed Report

U.S. ASSISTANCE
TO THE STATE OF ISRAEL

Prepared by the Staff of the
U.S. GENERAL ACCOUNTING OFFICE

DIGEST

The United States has furnished assistance to Israel since 1948.

—Aid levels have increased significantly since 1973 and in fiscal year 1982 exceeded $2 billion Foreign Military Sales (FMS) and Economic Support Fund (ESF).

—Following the 1979 Camp David Accords, Israel remained the largest recipient of U.S. economic and military security assistance and Egypt became the second largest.

The size of this program, along with its interaction with military assistance and arms sales to other countries in the important Middle East region led GAO to review the security assistance and related programs for Israel. The review covered justifications for assistance, its use, and its contributions to U.S. and Israeli interests and objectives. This is one of a continuing series of GAO reviews of assistance programs and security commitments with recipient countries.

The U.S. commitment to Israel has a long history dating back to President Truman's recognition of Israel on May 14, 1948. This commitment is predicated upon Israel's value as a strategic asset in that region of the world. Additionally, support for Israel is rooted in shared cultural, religious, and political values. The commitment is not couched in terms of any specific agreement such as a mutual security pact and the United States has followed a policy of step-by-step diplomacy in seeking to resolve various issues.

Spiraling Arms Transfers to the Middle East

The major objectives of U.S. assistance to Israel include demonstrating U.S. political support for an ally and providing for the defense of Israel. At the same time, however, the United States has a variety of interests in assisting Arab states in the Middle East and arms transfers to these Arab states are increasing as well.

As arms transfers to Arab states increase, Israeli officials believe that it must contend with the possibility of fighting nations which have acquired additional and improved equipment. As a result, perceptions of Israel's arms needs increase and this contributes to a spiraling arms transfer effect in the Middle East. **For example, the sale of AWACs and F-15 enhancements to Saudi Arabia led to an increase in FMS assistance to Israel.**

Precedent Setting Features of Israeli Program

Besides the size of the program, Israel has asked the United States for, and has already received to some degree, assistance under liberalized financing methods. Were these liberalized terms not provided, additional assistance may have been requested.

GAO takes no position on the level or terms of assistance to Israel but believes the precedents being set by the liberalized financing methods should be continually considered against the possibility that other recipient countries will ask for similar concessions. A few examples of granted liberalized financing techniques follow:

—Israel was the first beneficiary of the cash flow method of financing which allows a country to set aside only the amount of money needed to meet the current year's cash requirement for multi-year production contracts rather than the full amount. Egypt and Turkey were subsequently authorized use of the cash flow method. This has allowed the countries to stretch buying power and place more orders than the available loans authorized in a given year. It appears to GAO that this implies a commitment for the Congress to approve large financing programs in future years to ensure that signed contracts are honored.

—Israel has been forgiven (allowed write off) of a substantial portion of the FMS loan program ($750 million of $1.7 billion for fiscal year 1983). Now other countries have received the same benefit (Egypt and Sudan). Israel has also requested and received the forgiven portion of the FMS loans before drawing down on the interest bearing repayable part of the loans. This defers interest expenses for the Israeli Government.

—Israel will receive an ESF grant totaling $785 million in fiscal year 1983, making it the largest program recipient. Funds are provided to Israel as a cash transfer, not tied to development projects as in the case for most other countries.

—Israel receives trade offset arrangements from U.S. firms when it makes FMS purchases. Offsets are commitments by U.S. firms to purchase a specified amount of Israeli goods or services. Such arrangements are common under commercial arms sales but unusual under FMS.

Israel, more than any other FMS recipient country, has been provided with a higher level of military technologies having export potential. This could adversely impact on the U.S. economy and can affect U.S. ability to control proliferation of these technologies.

Israel has also asked for additional concessions to assist in further stretching its assistance. For example:

—Israel has asked that it and other FMS recipient countries be allowed to purchase Israeli goods with FMS credits. The request is pending. Normally FMS credits are used for purchases in the United States.

—Israel requested in 1982 that ESF funds be disbursed in a single payment at the beginning of the year. This would cost the U.S. Government in excess of $40 million in interest annually when compared to the usual quarterly disbursement of ESF funds. This is currently done only for Turkey, as part of an understanding with other donors, and no action has been taken on this request.

Financing Israel's Increasing Requirements

Even though large amounts of the FMS loans for Israel have been forgiven, there remains a large loan element. Debt servicing of these loans has become burdensome to Israel and this burden will increase in the near future. In 1982, Israel repaid the United States $875 million, most of which was for interest and principal on outstanding FMS loans. For the first time this was more than the cash transfer to Israel through the ESF program. Based on the current levels of assistance, the difference between ESF and the security assistance repayments will continue to increase — from $189 million in fiscal year 1983 to approximately $955 million in fiscal year 1993.

The United States and Israel are thus faced with the problem of how to finance the increasing requirement for new purchases as well as the repayments of outstanding loans.

Some Questions Facing the United States

Overall, the United States is faced with questions regarding the assistance program for Israel, along with other countries, that are not easily resolved. Among these are:

1. What is the impact of U.S. programs and policies on the spiraling Middle East arms escalation?

2. To what extent do concessions to Israel make it difficult to resist other recipients who might ask for similar concessions and what are the potential impacts and increased costs to the United States?

3. To what extent might Israel ask for increased U.S. assistance levels and concessions to be able to repay mounting debt servicing requirements to the United States?

CONTENTS

Chapter 1

Introduction

The continuity of the U.S.-Israeli relationship is a key tenet of U.S. policy in the Middle East. Towards that end, Israel as a stable democracy and the region's strongest military power, is considered by the United States to be a strategic asset. Nonetheless, some problems have surfaced regarding the relationship as the United States has attempted to reconcile its commitment to Israel with its other commitments and interests in the Middle East. Meanwhile, U.S. assistance programs for the defense of Israel have steadily increased and each U.S. President has restated the strong U.S. support for Israel.

U.S. Assistance to Israel

U.S. assistance to Israel from 1948 through fiscal year 1982 totaled over $24 billion. This includes
—about $16 billion in military loans and grants;
—about $6 billion in economic assistance loans and grants under the security assistance program; and
—over $2 billion in other nonsecurity assistance programs which include Food for Peace, housing guarantees, Export-Import Bank loans, and aid for resettling Jews from the Soviet Union.

Since 1974, almost half of Israel's military assistance has been in the form of grants and since 1975, economic aid has been a cash transfer, meaning that funds are not linked to specific programs or commodity imports. However, Israel is required to non-defense goods from the United States as it receives from economic aid.

U.S. military assistance to Israel exceeds assistance to any other country and continues to rise. At $1.7 billion, the fiscal year 1983 Foreign Military Sales (FMS) level is 21 percent above 1982, larger than for any other FMS recipient. The level for economic assistance, in the form of the Economic Support Fund (ESF), is $785 million which is also more than any other recipient.

U.S. Commitment to Israel

The United States has a commitment to Israel's continued national existence. This commitment is predicated not only upon Israel's value as a strategic asset but upon U.S. friendship with Israel which dates back to when President Truman recognized Israel on May 14, 1948. Additionally it is rooted in shared cultural, religious, and political values. The commitment is not couched in terms in any specific agreement such as a mutual security pact and the United States has followed a policy of step-by-step diplomacy in seeking to resolve various issues.

U.S. Role In the Middle East

The United States and Israel are in general agreement concerning the nature and extent of the Soviet threat to the region. However, the Israeli Government is concerned about U.S. efforts to assist various Arab countries to improve their military forces and thus achieve a strategic consensus against the threat of Soviet intrusion into the region. **Israeli officials believe that another war with the Arab countries is likely and that the U.S. regional efforts can contribute to threatening Israel security.**

Every U.S. President from Truman to Reagan has been involved in the formidable task of reconciling the Arab–Israeli conflict. Peace in the Middle East would remove many of the pressures and tensions on the United States in trying to serve its common interest with some of these countries but which for years have been engaged in internal regional conflicts. On the one hand, the United States has not yielded from its commitment to assist Israel to maintain its economic health and qualitative military superiority. At the same time, however, the United States has sought to increase friendly relations with various Arab nations who continue to resist the recognition of Israel as a nation. Certain Arab nations, such as Saudi Arabia, are an important source of oil for the United States, Western Europe, and Japan. Other Arab countries in the Middle East serve to check what the United States perceives as Soviet expansion in the region.

The United States has participated in a succession of diplomatic efforts to help the seemingly intractable Arab-Israeli conflict. This role escalated in 1975 when the United States agreed to act as "the eyes and ears of peace" by setting up an all-volunteer civilian watch in the Sinai. The United States played a major role in promoting peace in the Middle East through a settlement between Israel and Egypt at the Camp David Summit in September 1978, followed by a formal peace treaty in March 1979.

In the summer of 1982, President Reagan set forth his Middle East initiative to be a fresh start in the peace process and to reaffirm an ironclad U.S. commitment to Israel's security although **it included concerns for**

certain Israel actions. This was predicated on particular events which had taken place over the three intervening years since the Camp David Accords. The administration recognized that little progress was being made in normalizing Israeli-Arab relations. Secondly, it was the U.S. **belief that Israel had broken its assurances to the United States that it would not invade Beirut, Lebanon.** Finally, it was believed that Israel's continued settlements in the West Bank and Gaza and the continued U.S. silence on this issue, gave the impression of tacit endorsement of Israeli actions.

Objectives, Scope, and Methodology

The objectives of the review were to examine the full range of assistance to Israel and the U.S. policies which govern this relationship. Specific issues addressed were:

—The relationship which exists between the United States and Israel, and how this relationship is translated into policy objectives.

—The major determinants of aid levels to Israel and the extent to which there is information within the U.S. Government as to the use of these funds.

—The effect of U.S. aid on Israel's economy and is it meeting U.S. and Israeli objectives.

—The full range, status, implementation, and impact of the U.S. commitments to developing the Israeli arms industry—current and proposed.

—The use of funds and support provided to Israel pursuant to the Camp David Accords and the initial operations of the Multinational Force and Observers.

Scope

We conducted our review at the Departments of State, Defense, the Treasury, and Commerce; the Office of Management and Budget; the Central Intelligence Agency; and the Agency for International Development; and the American Embassy in Tel Aviv, Israel. We also obtained relevant data from and interviewed responsible Israeli officials from the Israeli Embassy, Washington, D.C.; the Israeli Military Procurement Mission, New York, N.Y.; the Ministries of Foreign Affairs, Defense (including component services), and Finance; and the Knesset. We also interviewed U.S. and Israeli industry representatives involved in defense industries.

Methodology

In the course of the review, we

—examined pertinent laws, regulations, and instructions;

—conducted literature searches;

—obtained and reviewed appropriate State, DOD, and private sector studies and reports;

—interviewed appropriate U.S. and Israeli military and civilian officials;

—visited selected Israeli defense industries and interviewed appropriate officials;

—reviewed files and records in order to obtain relevant data at all levels visited; and

—conducted pertinent economic and statistical analyses of U.S. financial assistance programs to Israel.

The review was carried out in accordance with generally accepted government auditing standards. Information relative to any threat assessment, Israel's defense posture, and the needs of Israeli armed forces were accepted from responsible U.S. and Israeli officials without verification. The rationale and reasons for the Israeli assistance program were accepted as set forth by the responsible U.S. officials.

Chapter 2

Foreign Military Sales

Foreign military sales to Israel, the largest U.S. military aid program, serves two major purposes. One is to indicate U.S. political support for Israel and the other is to ensure the security of Israel by providing military equipment for its defense needs.

Israeli military needs and U.S. political influences are both factors which determine FMS levels. The administration does evaluate Israeli military requirements, and the Congress also plays an important role. The Congress places more attention and exerts more influence on assistance to Israel than on other assistance programs.

Although its military has never been more modern and capable, Israel believes it has continuing modernization needs because of a potential Arab threat. Israel uses its FMS assistance for modern weapon acquisitions and other defense imports from the United States. Increasing U.S. and Soviet arms sales to other Middle East countries has led to a spiraling effect on weapons sales and assistance levels.

The United States supports Israeli plans for its forces modernization, and agrees that there is an Arab threat to Israel. **While Israel perceives the threat to be grave, DOD officials believe that it is overemphasized at this time. DOD believes that Israeli force modernization can be met at levels of $1.4 billion annually whereas Israel believes it needs higher levels of military assistance.**

The relationship is also exemplified by flexible terms and conditions for Israeli procurements with FMS assistance. Israel obtains more grants than any other recipient, has long term loans and is allowed to order military equipment under special financing arrangements before full funding is authorized by the Congress. Furthermore, during fiscal year 1982, it had been authorized to obtain its grant funds before its loan funds for military purchases—this allows Israel to defer for many years interest payments of approximately $19 million. Moreover, it also has used U.S.-furnished weapons in a manner, which the administration has stated, may have violated the purpose for which they were granted.

Development of Military Assistance to Israel

The United States has had a formal military assistance relationship with Israel since 1952, but did not become its major supplier of arms until after the June War of 1967. The annual large U.S. military assistance program began after the October War of 1973. In 1962, some U.S. military loans were made and in 1966, the United States agreed to ensure the sales of arms to Israel, if not from Western sources, then from the United States. Hawk air defense missiles and A4 fighters were sold to Israel but the major suppliers of military equipment remained the British for tanks and the French for aircraft. After the Six Day War of 1967, France discontinued its aircraft sales and the United States began sales of the F-4 aircraft. U.S. military assistance to Israel totaled more than $1.4 billion for fiscal years 1950 through 1973. Since 1973, this assistance has significantly increased as shown in Appendix 2.

FMS Assistance Levels for Israel

Since 1974, Israel has been the recipient of more FMS assistance than any other country. Through fiscal years 1974 to 1982, Israel received almost $13.5 billion in FMS assistance. Of this total, $5.4 billion was in the form of grants while about $8 billion was in long term loans. In fiscal year 1982, Israel obtained $1.4 billion in FMS financing which was 35 percent of the total U.S. military assistance program. Egypt obtained $900 million while all other recipients received less than $1.7 billion.

The administration proposed increasing Israeli FMS to $1.7 billion for fiscal year 1983 and Egyptian FMS to $1.3 billion. The Israeli program was proposed to include a grant element of $500 million and long term loans for the other $1.2 billion. The Congress approved $1.7 billion FMS assistance to Israel with a grant element of $750 million.

According to the Central Intelligence Agency (CIA), Israeli expectations are that the United States will fund half of its defense budget. Israeli documents show that U.S. assistance funded 37 percent of its defense budget for fiscal year 1982.

Assistance levels appear to react to political events, as shown in the chart (See Appendix 2), which portrays the interplay of events and increases in Israel's levels of FMS assistance. The levels stabilized at $1 billion per annum during fiscal years 1977 to 1980, except for $2.2 billion specifically allocated in 1979 for withdrawal from the Sinai. Otherwise, FMS assistance rose above the general trend in two circumstances. The first time was for Israeli rearmament after the October 1973 war when FMS assistance reached $2.5 billion in fiscal year 1974. The second was when Israel obtained $1.7 billion in loans and grants in fiscal year 1976, after Israel's second disengagement in the Sinai.

Israel experienced difficulties meeting payments for procurements in 1981 and requested an additional $200 million in FMS. The administration agreed, and made the request to the Congress, which added another $200 million and the FMS assistance level rose to $1.4 billion for fiscal year 1981. This same amount of assistance was continued into fiscal year 1982. **In fiscal year 1983, due to the sale of the Airborne Warning and Control System (AWACS) and F-15 aircraft enhancements to Saudi Arabia, the administration requested a new level of $1.7 billion in FMS assistance and plans this level through fiscal year 1984. Oficials in DOD and State Department believe that due to Congressional interest — $1.7 billion may become the new minimum for FMS to Israel.**

Congressional Role

The Congress consistently views administration aid proposals for Israel favorably, and in recent years, has appropriated more aid for Israel than the President requested. The Congress has earmarked Israeli security assistance to provide Economic Support Fund (ESF) on a cash basis, included larger amounts of forgiven FMS loans, and granted favorable repayment terms for arms purchases. For example, for fiscal year 1982, the Congress approved $50 million more in FMS grants than the administration requested. Again for fiscal year 1983, the Congress approved $750 million in FMS grants although the administration had proposed only $500 million in grants.

State and DOD officials say that it is not politically possible to submit to the Congress, as an administration proposal, a lower FMS figure for Israel than that for the previous fiscal year. The perception held by some DOD and State officials is that congressional approval for FMS is easier to obtain if increases to Israeli assistance are sought.

Foreign Policy Considerations

Many consider FMS assistance as a policy of U.S. support for Israel. **State Department officials noted that reduction in the program could trigger a crisis in political relations between Israel and the United States. Arab States, as well as other countries and world institutions, might perceive that U.S. support for Israel is waning if FMS levels were to be reduced. If the United States stopped providing FMS to Israel the consequences could be a halt to the peace process, a deterioration of Israeli military forces and economic difficulties leading to a request for military debt rescheduling.**

We were told that decisions regarding FMS are made at the highest levels of the administration. **Justifying FMS for Israel is seen only as an exercise by some lower ranking executive branch officials.** The assistance levels are determined by policy considerations beyond those involving only basic defense needs.

FMS to Israel linked with Egypt

The Egyptian and Israeli FMS assistance programs are politically tied to each other and are becoming more difficult to separate. The Egyptians have been requesting treatment similar to the Israeli since Camp David. This is reflected in higher levels of assistance, similar terms of FMS repayment, similar desires for advanced equipment, and similar uses of cash flow, and similar desires for advanced equipment. [sic] **The Israelis, on the other hand, desire that the United States maintain its special relationship which means favorable treatment. In Israeli eyes, the linkage is eroding part of their special relationship.**

Israeli Military Needs

U.S. and Israeli officials agree that Israel has security problems which require FMS assistance. However, there is growing concern in Israel over the level of FMS due to: increasing U.S. arms sales to Arab countries; erosion of its qualitative advantage; and Israeli force modernization needs. **Nonetheless, DOD officials generally believe current FMS levels are sufficient for Israel's needs.**

Effect of other U.S. Middle East arms sales and assistance

U.S. arms sales and FMS assistance to Israel are not only linked to Egypt but also to certain other Arab countries who have or can get the funds to pay for these arms. Arms sales to an Arab state in the region generally have led to another sale to Israel or increased FMS to offset Israeli security concerns. This, Soviet sales, and the floor effect have resulted in spiral of arms sales to the region and assistance levels.

Current controversy in arms sales to the Arabs began with the sale of F-15 aircraft to Saudi Arabia in 1978. When the administration presented its case for the sale, it said this was not a single sale but a package of aircraft sales to the three Middle East countries, with 15 F-15 and 75 F-16 aircraft going to Israel, 60 F-15 aircraft to Saudi Arabia, and 50 F-5E aircraft to Egypt. The Carter administration said the package approach enhanced U.S. interests in the region and those of all three recipient countries. It also helped ensure the security of Israel, which opposed the sale of the F-15 aircraft to the Saudis, by helping to maintain the balance of Arab and Israeli air forces in the Middle East region. The administration linked the sales to the three countries so that it was more difficult for the Congress to isolate action on the Saudi F-15 aircraft sale from action on the aircraft sales to Egypt and Israel.

The sale of AWACS and F-15 aircraft enhancements to Saudi Arabia also led to an increase in FMS assistance to Israel. The administration testified that the extra $300 million of FMS assistance for Israel was for its security needs and not specifically because of the AWACS sale to Saudi Arabia. However, we found that the State Department planned to request $300 million in extra FMS for Israel for fiscal years 1983 and 1984 if the sale of AWACS and F-15 aircraft enhancements went through the Congress. These extra funds would be for F-15 aircraft or additional Israeli discretionary procurements.

Administration officials informally admit that F-15 aircraft enhancements and AWACS to Saudi Arabia resulted in more FMS to Israel. They also speculate that sales of I-Hawk missile and F-16 aircraft to Jordan could have similar effects of increasing FMS to Israel. Israel takes a pessimistic view of the trend of U.S. arms sales to Arab countries and fears that the focus of U.S. regional concern is shifting toward the Persian Gulf and Saudi Arabia. **The effect on Israel is to reinforce its desire to protect its special relationship with the United States and try to limit U.S. arms sales to the Arab States.**

Israeli concerns for threat from region

Israelis are particularly sensitive to the level of casualties they might sustain in a full-scale war with the Arabs. **The efforts to modernize Arab States such as Saudi Arabia and Jordan to improve their military capability to meet threats from Iran and Syria and to deter Soviet expansion also expand the Arabs' potential capability against Israel. CIA believes this could exacerbate Israeli concerns about the Arab threat and could foster Israeli preemptive attacks in future crises.** Although some of Israel's potential adversaries are obtaining the same generation of technologically advanced weapons, U.S. officials point out that Israel retains greater operational effectiveness of its forces. This is attributable to superior leadership, morale, training, motivation, and the ability to employ and maintain advanced technology weapons, acquisition and integration of command, control, and intelligence systems complement Israel's ability to employ its forces more effectively than the Arab States. **CIA, however, notes that the numbers and quality of weapons and support systems likely to enter Arab inventories and their improved availability to use them may gradually begin to narrow Israel's qualitative edge near the end of the 1980s.**

Some State Department officials believe that the qualitative gap is already getting smaller between Israel and the Arabs and agree that U.S. assistance is helping to narrow the gap. DOD analysts point out that the methodology in determining qualitative edge is not precise and that it is difficult to determine what exactly tips the balance. **DOD officials stress, however, Israel's ability to use the equipment more effectively and that it has always defeated the Arabs. Thus, DOD officials noted that, although U.S. arms sales do represent problems for Israel, it can maintain its qualitative advantage. Moreover, the President has assured Israel that he is determined to see that it maintains its qualitative technological edge.**

Differences in view of the threat

In general, U.S. officials agree that the Middle East is a very unstable area and will continue to be so for the foreseeable future. Both countries agree that there are Arab States which pose a potential threat to Israel. However, the United States does not concur with all Israeli assessments concerning the threat.

Israel views its immediate threat as the military forces of **the combined armies of Syria and Jordan, aligned with additional forces from Saudi Arabia, Iraq, and the other Arab countries. Syria and Jordan are seen as direct confrontational states, as well as Saudi Arabia. Iraq poses less immediate concern for Israel but it expects a substantial Iraqi presence in any potential conflict. According to Israeli military planners, Egypt remains a potential threat. Israel says it has to have an Egyptian scenario because the treaty has not been sufficiently tested by time and events and the unstable character of Arab governments in the Middle East.**

The balance of military forces between the Arabs and Israel is considered to remain in the Arabs' favor by Israeli military planners. Additional Israeli concern is voiced over Western and Soviet weapon systems sold to the Arabs.

The United States believes Israel faces less of an Arab threat. The U.S. position is that there are moderate Arab states which include Egypt, Jordan, and Saudi Arabia. However, Israel does not agree that these are moderate Arab States. CIA estimated that another combined Arab-Israeli War is unlikely in the near future because of (1) the general disarray in the Arab world and the effects of the Iran-Iraq War, and (2) weapons ratios are now better for Israel that they were in the October War in 1973.

Although Israeli military planners informed us that they could defend Israel with weapons ratios that were 3 to 1 against them, they noted that the combined Arab weapons inventories exceed this ratio. U.S. officials point out that Israeli military projections are unrealistic in that they include every weapon in all the Arab countries as part of the ratio of arms lined up against Israel.

The following chart shows the CIA estimate of a present worst-case military balance as of April 1982.

[7 PAGES OF TEXT WERE NOT AVAILABLE]

. . . other DOD officials said that there will probably be more sales of the captured equipment.

Conclusion

There are differences between the United States and Israel regarding the perceived threat to Israel and its military needs. Joint planning groups have been established with other Middle East countries to determine their military needs and to resolve differences such as are present regarding Israel. However, considering the other influencing factors, which we discussed above, it is likely that establishment of such a group for Israel would have limited effect.

FMS Financing Flexibility

The U.S. relationship with Israel is exemplified by the more liberal terms, conditions, and purchasing flexibility of FMS assistance. Israel receives more FMS forgiven loans than any other recipient, more FMS loans with long term repayment periods and its procurement of military systems has been expanded through an administrative mechanism called cash flow financing.

FMS forgiven loans

In the fiscal year 1983 program, $750 million of the FMS loans for Israel were designated as forgiven and do not have to be repaid. Egypt was also allocated $425 million in forgiven credits. Forgiveness of FMS loans to Israel has continued throughout the past decade. The United States has forgiven part of the FMS loans provided to Israel which, in effect, makes these funds grants. From 1976 through 1980, not including Camp David, the forgiven portion of the loans usually reflected one-half the level of FMS assistance for that year. After FMS assistance passed the $1 billion level in 1981, the figure $500 million was substituted in lieu of "one-half" the FMS assistance level. The forgiveness portion was increased by Congress to $550 million in 1982.

For fiscal year 1983, the administration had proposed forgiving $500 million of a total $1.7 billion FMS package for Israel. Israel has requested a return to the formula of one-half loan for its FMS assistance. Under the continuing resolution for fiscal year 1983, the Congress approved $750 million of forgiven FMS credits out of the $1.7 billion FMS assistance package.

FMS loan repayment

Israel has long term repayment of 30 years on its FMS loans, in contrast to what has been the usual repayment period of 13 years to most recipients. Conditions of repayment are a 10-year grace period on repayment of principal. Interest rates for FMS loans are based on interest rates charged the U.S. Treasury for its outstanding marketable obligations plus a nominal administrative fee. In addition to Israel, other countries now allowed these more liberal repayment terms for FMS loans include Egypt, Greece, Somalia, Sudan, and Turkey.

Cash flow financing

In addition to liberal terms for repayment of FMS assistance, Israel also has more flexibility in the procurement of U.S. military goods than almost all other FMS recipients. This flexibility is referred to as cash flow financing. In effect, it allows Israel to order military equipment based on future FMS expectations which have not yet been authorized by Congress.

It has been allowed to use this financing method since 1974. Egypt was permitted cash flow privileges after Camp David and, more recently, Turkey also was granted cash flow for certain FMS procurements. As we reported in 1982, cash flow financing implies a strong commitment by the

United States to provide large amounts of credit in future years, limiting, in our view, the prerogatives of the Congress in authorizing the U.S. security assistance program.

When a weapons system is purchased, the buyer signs an agreement specifying the dates of equipment deliveries and the payment schedule. While the total cost of an item may be tens or hundreds of millions of dollars, not all of the money will be paid in the first year after the contract is signed. Major systems have a long lead time before delivery, usually several years, and payments will be spread out over this time period.

Under normal FMS financing procedures, the United States requires that the buyer reserve, or set aside, the full cost of the item when the order is placed. This means that if an item costs $100 million, FMS credits of $100 million must be set aside when the agreement is signed, even though actual payments may be made years later. This is to ensure that a country will have all the funds necessary to pay for the item it has ordered.

With the cash flow system, however, the country sets aside only the amount of money needed to meet the current fiscal year's cash requirements. The payment schedule for a $100 million item, for example, may require that only $50 million be paid the first year. Under the cash flow system, Israel can set aside only $50 million and use the other $50 million to place additional orders. Thus Israel expects to get from FMS credits to be authorized the following year by the U.S. Congress, the money it needs to meet its second year $50 million payment. Should Congress not authorize these credits, Israel nevertheless would remain contractually bound to pay the $50 million due the second year from other monies available to it. As a practical matter, however, it is unlikely that the Congress would refuse to authorize FMS credits sufficient for Israel to meet its contractual obligations. This could severely limit the flexibility of the Congress in authorizing future FMS credit programs.

Israel used cash flow financing during fiscal years 1976 through 1980 to pay for the procurement of its initial F-16 aircraft.

The following chart shows the existing obligations, as of December 1982, made on future FMS procurements for Israel through this method. (See Appendix 3)

Defense Security Assistance Agency (DSAA) monitors the cash flow concept and ensures that Israel has sufficient FMS funds to make the necessary periodic payments on its cash flow purchases. As a result of its major equipment purchases during fiscal years 1977-1979 under cash flow, Israel could not make any major equipment procurements during fiscal year 1981, because too many funds were already committed. Furthermore, as is discussed in Chapter 5, we found that during 1980, funds provided for the Sinai redeployment were authorized for use to cover Israel shortfalls in cash flow financing needs.

Conclusion

Although DOD officials point out that there is no U.S. commitment for future Israel procurements due to the cash flow system, we believe it does imply a strong commitment that the Congress will finance large programs in future years for Israel. Because the use of this method of financing can limit Congressional prerogatives in reviewing and authorizing FMS credit levels, we recommended in our February 1982 report on Egypt that the Secretaries of State and Defense fully disclose to the Congress the rationale and the implications of cash flow authorizations for Egypt and Israel.

We also recommended that the Congress amend the Arms Export Control Act (AECA) to require advance notification by the executive branch when cash flow financing is to be authorized for selected countries. However, these recommendations have not been adopted.

Israeli FMS drawdowns

Under an Office of Management and Budget (OMB) policy, a country must draw down proportionally on its FMS loans and grants rather than drawing down on grants prior to FMS loans. The policy applies to all recipients obtaining $100 million or more in U.S. military assistance.

OMB and Treasury officials say that a proportional drawdown policy equalizes interest benefits and penalties between an FMS recipient and the United States. State and DSAA officials, however, are opposed to such a policy. Their objection is based on an administration position to minimize the debt burdens on security assistance recipients.

It is to Israel's advantage to draw down on FMS grant funds first and guaranteed loans later and thereby postpone interest payments on its FMS loans. Israel previously was permitted to draw down its FMS grant funds prior to its loans and both it and Egypt did this during fiscal year 1982. This proportionally greater and earlier drawdown of FMS grants by Israel, during fiscal year 1982, allowed Israel to defer until many years later an estimated $19 million in interest repayments.

There is disagreement in the administration as to when the policy was implemented. Treasury and OMB officials maintain that the policy was

initiated in 1979, but DSAA officials claim that it did not appear until March 1982. The State Department did issue an action memorandum implementing a proportional drawdown policy for Israel in January 1982. However, due to budget delays and foreign policy considerations both Israel and Egypt draw down on FMS grants before FMS loans.

The State Department's Undersecretary for Security Assistance, Science and Technology reaffirmed the policy on October 21, 1982, for all FMS recipients obtaining $100 million or more of assistance. State's confirmation of the proportional drawdown policy contains an exception that if the policy is broken, e.g., by Congressional action on Israel, other countries will not be held to it either.

There appears to have been a firm policy for all FMS recipients until fiscal year 1983. The policy, when viewed solely from a budgetary aspect, should result in economic savings to the United States. State Department's general rule, that negates the policy for all recipients if there is an exception for one, actually would apply to Egypt and Israel under the current program and thus seems to be a practical step to reduce pressure to change the policy for either.

U.S. Enforcement of Arms Sales Controls

A 1952 agreement between Israel and the United States provides that defense articles and services sold to Israel may be used only for certain purposes, such as internal security and legitimate self-defense. Although sanctions for substantial violation of these restrictions are imposed by section 3 of the AECA, the Act authorized but does not require the President to determine that a substantial violation has occurred. It only requires that the President report to the Congress upon receipt of information that a violation "may have occurred." Section 3 sanctions may also be imposed if the Congress determines by joint resolution that a substantial violation has occurred.

Although the President has reported to the Congress at least four times that a violation may have occurred with respect to Israel, neither he nor the Congress has ever determined that Israel was in substantial violation in using weapons for an unauthorized purpose. If such a determination were made by the Congress, credits and guarantees to Israel would be cut off, as well as cash sales and deliveries under previous sales. If the determination were made by the President, he could certify that a termination of arms sales to Israel would have "significant adverse impact" on U.S. security. This would permit deliveries under previous arms sales contracts to continue, but still would cut off the use of FMS credits and guarantees for payment.

In March 1978, Israeli military forces crossed into southern Lebanon. The Israeli government characterized its military operation as limited self-defense against a pattern of attacks from Lebanon carried out by Palestinians and directed against Israeli civilians. By letter dated April 5, 1978, Secretary of State Cyrus Vance reported to the Congress that "a violation of the 1952 Agreement may have occurred by reason of the Israeli operations in Lebanon." In view of a statement by the Government of Israel that it intended to comply with U.N. Security Council Resolution 425 which called for Israeli withdrawal from Lebanon, the Secretary of State said he was not recommending that the President take any further action.

In 1979, Israeli forces again crossed into Lebanon and U.S.-supplied Israeli aircraft bombed "Palestinian targets" in southern Lebanon. By letter of August 6, 1979, Secretary of State Cyrus Vance reported "that a violation of the 1952 Agreement may have occurred by reason of such actions as Israel's July 22 air strikes and the deployment in Southern Lebanon of U.S.-supplied artillery subject to U.S. law."

Similarly, in 1981, the Secretary of State reported to Congress that a violation of the 1952 agreement may have occurred, by reason of Israel's air attack on Iraqi nuclear facilities. In the case of Israel's 1982 invasion of Lebanon, the continued bombing of Beirut and the use by Israel of cluster bombs, the Secretary of State again reported that a violation of the 1952 Agreement "may have occurred."

The language of the Arms Export Control Act itself is responsible chiefly for the lack of Presidential determinations of whether or not a substantial violation has occurred. Under section 3 (c) (2), the President must report whenever he receives information that a violation "may have occurred." In each prior case, the President has followed this statutory language literally in reporting to the Congress. The Act does not require that he do anything more.

Under the AECA, the Congress also could have determined by joint resolution that Israel was in substantial violation of restrictions on the use of U.S.-supplied weapons. However, the Congress need not pass such a joint resolution nor has it done so.

A definitive determination of a violation would implement the sanctions of the AECA. The sanctions would cut off U.S. assistance and arms sales as was the case during the previous embargo for Turkey over the Cyprus affair. However, taking such a step in Israel's case is something that administration officials and the Congress have been reluctant to do. They have pointed out that such extreme measures could cause a crisis in the relationship between the two countries. **The State Department informed us that, as a general rule, it does not believe that such sanctions or restrictions are effective mechanisms for achieving peace in the Middle East.**

Review and Oversight of Israeli Procurements

Since 1952, Israel has operated a military procurement mission in New York City. It is in charge of procurements from the United States and controls 40 percent of Israel's annual defense budget. In 1981, for example, the Mission used FMS financing to purchase $1.4 billion in U.S. defense goods —both from commercial sources and through direct FMS procurement.

The Mission informed us that it makes around 30,000 purchases per year, of which 1,000 are for direct FMS sales and 29,000 are for commercial purchases using FMS funds. We were told that about 100 purchases are for more than $1 million while 85 percent are for less than $5,000.

The Munitions Control Office at the State Department issues export licenses for commercial procurements of military items. Its officials said that the Israeli procurement lists have been preapproved. **The philosophy at Munitions Control is that there is little reason to refuse any export license for goods to Israel.**

DSAA also handles the Israeli program differently from other countries. With other country programs, DSAA reviews all invoices but has deviated from this policy for Israel, due to the volume. For Israel, DSAA reviews all purchases of $50,000 to $500,000 after they are issued but all commercial contracts using FMS assistance of $500,000 or more require preapproval of DSAA.

An arrangement was reached in 1981, whereby the Mission submits all invoices over $100,000 to DSAA and promises to maintain and submit computer reports to its purchasers. DSAA also may randomly request any invoice for sample review. Officials at DSAA say that they review 4 to 5 sample invoices a week and that they have not found any improper purchases.

Chapter 3

Israel's Economy and the U.S. Assistance

The United States has expressed its support to Israel, in addition to FMS financial assistance, through the Economic Support Fund (ESF). Besides being the largest program, ESF aid to Israel is also provided under liberal terms. The program, since 1981, has been an all grant transfer of cash provided to support the Israeli economy and help the country address its balance of payments problems.

None of the ESF aid to Israel is tied to development projects, as is the case for ESF provided to almost all of the other recipient countries. Therefore, the amount is not based on a specific developmental need and there is no way to measure the precise effects that these funds have on Israel's economy. Rather, these funds serve a budget support and political purpose.

Israeli officials recently sought earlier release of ESF funds which have traditionally been disbursed quarterly. This would enable Israel to have earlier use of the funds but at an annual cost of more than $40 million to the U.S. Treasury.

Israel continues to experience economic problems associated with inflation and its balance of payments. However, according to Israeli officials, it has been able to meet its debt servicing obligations, regularly increase its reserves, and expand exports. This is a considerable accomplishment given the country's large defense burden while absorbing over one million immigrants since its beginning as a country. These accomplishments are made possible, to a great extent, by U.S. economic assistance which has been a major source of funds to help the country meet its balance of payment deficit. Also, as noted in Chapter 2, 37 percent of Israel's defense needs in FY 1982 were provided through FMS loans and grants.

Although U.S. assistance has been large and provided under liberal terms, U.S. decisionmakers are now faced with an increasing dilemma in continuing to bolster Israel's economy and ensure support of its budget. For the first time, beginning in fiscal year 1982, ESF disbursements to Israel were less than Israeli military debt repayments. This net flow of funds from Israel to the United States under the Security Assistance Program will continue to grow in the 1980s and contribute to an overall increasing Israeli need for foreign currency. Consequently, it is likely that Israel will intensify its requests to the United States for increased assistance through such ways as increased amounts of ESF, forgiving or rescheduling current debt, better terms on future loans, and through U.S. assistance as consumers of Israeli products.

In addition to Israel's rising military debts and other problems, the United States is faced with the possibility of indirectly supporting Israeli actions, with which it does not necessarily agree, through the bolstering of Israeli budget needs. **Israeli officials maintain that the Lebanon campaign will not result in any increase in requests for U.S. assistance but U.S. reports speculate otherwise.** Furthermore, the Israeli government's liberal subsidies granted to its people for settling on the West Bank must be absorbed at the cost of other needs. We do not mean to imply that U.S. assistance, even though very substantial, gives the United States any right to dictate policies to other countries. Certainly many recipient countries sometimes carry out policies with which the United States does not wholly agree.

The United States Devotes Substantial Support to Israel's Economy

Between 1972 and 1982, the United States provided $5.9 billion, first under the Security Supporting Assistance program and currently under ESF. According to the Agency for International Development (AID), which administers the program, these funds provide direct support to Israel's economy by assisting the country to address its balance of payments deficit. Further, the assistance encourages economic stability in the face of the tremendous burden caused by the large percentage of resources devoted to defense.

The quantity and quality of U.S. economic support

The ESF program, which authorized about $2.5 billion in assistance worldwide during fiscal year 1982, is second in size to the FMS program among the five major security assistance programs.

As shown (in Appendix 4), only Egypt receives funds under the ESF program approximating those received by Israel.

Israel had been receiving a mix of ESF grants and loans until fiscal year 1981, when the Congress started authorizing all grants for the Israeli ESF program. The Congress has favored all grants since that time despite administration proposals to convert back to a mix of two-thirds grants and one-third loans. For fiscal year 1983, the Congress approved $785 million in ESF grants to Israel.

Appendix 5 depicts the levels of U.S. economic assistance since 1972. Israel receives this amount of economic assistance without having any designated development projects. Almost all other ESF recipient countries have at least some development projects tied to assistance. This is changing, and the degree of cash transfers is increasing but Israel was the first to receive a full cash transfer. Thus the Israeli program set a precedent to move this type assistance further away from economic development programs.

Israel is required to purchase an equivalent amount in non-defense goods from the United States as the condition of ESF. Beginning in fiscal year 1979, the conditions which required that Israel provide specific evidence of each non-military purchase were dropped. Instead, Israel was asked to ensure that (1) it will import from the United States a total amount of non-defense goods at least equal to the level of U.S. economic assistance, (2) U.S. exporters will continue to enjoy equal access to Israeli markets, and (3) it will follow procedures worked out in cooperation with the United States for bulk shipments of grain on dry bulk carriers.

Determination of ESF Levels

Since ESF aid to Israel is not tied to specific development projects, its purpose has been expressed by the administration in various ways such as to (1) maintain economic stability and a modest level of growth, (2) provide balance of payments support, and (3) import certain civilian goods and services without high cost commercial borrowing and foreign exchange reserve drawdowns.

Israel, in its latest aid request to the United States, requests that economic aid be granted at volumes sufficient to cover a major share of its financing gap of $1.2 billion. The request points out that whatever Israel cannot generate from its own resources or from U.S. assistance, it must obtain through short-term borrowing. **A recent CIA study points out, however,** that Israel could use its foreign exchange reserves or, if needed, could take further domestic austerity measures to decrease imports.

[additional material deleted from later draft.]

Because ESF is not project tied, the amount of aid is based on political considerations and some economic analysis. **The U.S. Embassy, in commenting on Israel's 1983 aid request, gave its view that continuance of aid at** the same levels as in fiscal year 1982 appeared to be the best course of action from both a political and economic point of view. While showing an undiminished U.S. support to Israel's creditors, the U.S. Embassy reported that the aid in real terms would be lower which might provide extra incentive for Israel's economic policymakers to restrict public as well as private consumption. In its assessment of Israel's fiscal year 1984 aid request, the Embassy essentially repeated these same views.

The Embassy felt that any reduction of ESF would be impractical both economically and politically. Economically, it was expressed that Israel's economic stabilization programs would be damaged and it would hurt the country's chances to obtain foreign exchange from commercial sources. Politically, it was believed that such an unprecedented occurrence would be interpreted as a reduction in overall U.S. support, could adversely impact on future peace efforts, and could affect broader U.S. goals in the entire region.

Continuing, the Embassy said that an increase in aid would assist Israel economically and demonstrate that, even with disagreements between countries, the United States has not changed its commitment to Israel. However, it believed that arguments against higher aid levels were more compelling. First, Israel could manage at current assistance levels. Secondly, increased aid would remove some of the urgency that exists for an economic austerity program. Also, increased levels might damage Israel's standing within U.S. public opinion where reductions were taking place in domestic U.S. programs and in other foreign aid programs.

The Congress has had much impact on ESF aid to Israel by revising the Administration's proposals. Based on AID's analysis of the state of the Israeli economy and debt repayment, the administration proposed that ESF be provided on a one-third loan and two-thirds grant basis for fiscal years 1981 and 1982. On both occasions, the Congress disagreed and provided the funds as a full grant. In the proposal for fiscal year 1983, the administration again recommended that ESF be provided at the same ratio of loan and grant as was previously proposed but the Congress approved a full grant.

It was proposed in the Senate to link ESF levels to Israel's annual debt repayment to the United States which is estimated to be $875 million in 1982 and growing. Almost all of this debt is related to prior military purchases and opponents of the linkage concept fear that this might serve only to increase military loan requests. In defeating this proposal, others pointed to the precedent-setting nature of such actions, which might cause other countries to seek similar arrangements. The Department of State felt that such a tie could result in the diversion of funds under the total authorization from other countries who have justifiable needs.

Israel seeks early release of funds

Traditionally, Israel has received ESF in quarterly cash transfers from AID. These funds become part of Israel's foreign exchange and can be spent without identity as U.S. aid. More recently, Israel has requested that all of the funds be disbursed at the beginning of each quarter. Although early release of ESF funds is only done for Turkey, and this is a special case per a U.S. understanding with other donor countries, Israel's request has been supported by the House Appropriations Committee. If ESF funds were released earlier, it would increase the interest costs for the United States because the U.S. Treasury would have to borrow the funds earlier. At the same time, releasing ESF earlier could be a corresponding benefit to Israel.

To ascertain the significance of this extra cost to the United States, we calculated the amount of interest that would have been involved for fiscal years 1981 and 1982, using interest rates provided by the Treasury Department. In fiscal year 1981, the ESF for Israel was $764 million and the additional interest charge to release these funds at the beginning of the fiscal year would have amounted to $46.3 million. In fiscal year 1982, the ESF amount was $806 million and the corresponding additional cost of early release would have been $41.5 million. Although a smaller amount of ESF was distributed to Israel during fiscal year 1981 than in 1982, the greater amount of interest reflects the higher market rates of interest charged during that year.

Conclusion

The costs to the U.S. Treasury for the earlier release of funds would be substantial. If AID, as the program administrator, or the Department of State, as the policymaker, agrees to release ESF funds earlier than on the traditional quarterly basis for any country, this should be done only with the full recognition of the extra cost to the United States.

Israel's Problems and Plans Related to Economic Development

In Israel's fiscal year (begins April, 1982), defense and debt repayment expenditures were estimated to be about 57 percent of its total budget. Its defense spending equated to an estimated 21.3 percent of its Gross National Product (GNP).

It is important to point out, however, that more than one-third of Israel's defense budget from 1977 to 1981 was funded by the United States, mostly through FMS grants and loans. The grants have no adverse impact on the Israeli economy while the loans have a 30-year term with a 10-year grace period on principal. Therefore, Israel, in effect, has been able to defer paying a large portion of its defense budget each year.

An Israeli official noted that, due to U.S. aid, Israel has been able to meet its debt-servicing obligations without fail, regularly increase its foreign reserves, and has expanded exports. Without U.S. aid, it is doubtful that Israel could have made these accomplishments given its tremendous defense investment. However, Israel's foreign reserve position, although growing in absolute terms, is declining as compared to its level of imports. In 1981, the reserves were sufficient to finance only 11 weeks of imports as compared to 16 weeks in 1973, according to Israeli statistics. **[Deletion made from later draft.]** Along with U.S. aid, Israel points to its reserve position as a major factor enabling it to borrow funds on the commercial market.

Israel's economic goals

Israel has an immediate goal to reduce the rate of its inflation and a longer term goal to effect a gradual decline in the current account deficit of the non-military balance of payments, which includes interest charges on military and nonmilitary debt. However, Israel estimates that military imports will rise so that its overall current deficit will not be reduced during its forecasting period through 1986. According to Israeli's current aid request to the United States:

"Economic policy in the coming years will be based on the concept of controlled and selective growth. The target is to stimulate the economy up to the level at which inflationary pressures can be kept under control. Growth will be led by an optimal increase in exports and a renewed upswing in investment, while the increase of private and public consumption will be restricted."

According to an Israeli Government official, the causes of these economic problems are the increased prices of oil, grain, and other imported products, the country's domestic growth and, of course, its very high military expenditures. Israel has been virtually operating in a wartime economy since its establishment as a state in 1948. Twenty percent of its work force is directly and indirectly employed by the military or in defense related industries. Of these, many are needed for service in Lebanon, the West Bank, Gaza and the Golan Heights. **For example, roughly 70,000 reservists were called up for the Lebanon incursion.**

Israel's rate of inflation has been more than that common in other industrial countries. In 1980, annual inflation was 132.9 percent, dropping to 101.5 percent during 1981, and was estimated to rise to about 125 percent during 1982. Israel has shielded its population from the effects of inflation through an indexing system that adjusts costs and payments to help keep pace, and subsidies to keep prices artificially low. **[Deletion made but from later draft.]** At the same time, Israel's strong unions have been able to extract real wage gains, thereby increasing demand for both domestic and imported products. With an increase in the domestic demand, Israeli manufacturers produce to satisfy these demands rather than producing for the export market.

In order to reach its longer term goal of continued reductions in its non-military balance of payments deficit, Israel seeks to improve export growth. **[Deletion made but from later draft.]** Historically, Israel has been very successful in this endeavor and, although it continues to experience a trade deficit, the rate of exports has increased faster than imports. As a result, the proportion of non-military imports financed by exports grew from 68 percent in 1973 to 84 percent in 1981. Viewed another way, Israel's non-military trade deficit was about 47 percent of exports in 1973 as compared to about 20 percent of exports in 1981.

Israel projects that, if it can implement its policies and if the world economy turns upwards, it will be able to increase annual exports by about 15.5 percent, realize an annual GNP growth of about 5 percent, and increase gross domestic investment growth by 7 percent. By sustaining such growth, Israel points to a projected net decline in its non-military balance of payments deficit from an estimated $2.7 billion in 1982 to $1.6 billion by 1986, a 44 percent reduction.

Overall, however, according to Israel's own figures, almost all of the reductions projected to occur in its non-military deficit will be consumed by increases in the country's direct military imports so that little change will occur in the overall deficit. Israel's published economic policies do not address this critical factor. An example of the problem is that according to Israeli officials, budget cuts were planned in the defense sector in fiscal year

1982, but because of the need for supplementary budgets due to the war in Lebanon, these cuts will not be realized.

U.S. assessment of Israeli goals

U.S. assessments cast doubt on Israel's ability to reach its economic goals as quickly as it anticipates. **According to a May 1981 report, the goals of reducing real spending and curbing real wage gains by Israel's unions are particularly important and equally difficult.**

The U.S. Embassy, in a more recent assessment of Israel's economic projects through 1986, also cast doubt on the availability of the country to realize the benefits associated with its "overly optimistic" analysis as quickly as anticipated. The worldwide recession prevented Israel from reaching its export goals in fiscal year 1982 and, although the country is capable of quickly shifting production to export markets, Israeli exports may not recover as rapidly as forecasted if the recovery of Western economies is slow.

The Embassy, in commenting on Israel's fiscal year 1983 aid request, proposed a determined U.S. effort to help Israel increase its exports as a way of eventually reducing aid levels. Since the United States has already taken some initial steps in the area of military exports (see Chapter 4), it recommended an examination of similar possibilities for civilian exports. Both countries obviously prefer to lessen Israel's dependence on direct U.S. assistance in return for an economically stronger Israel. However, for Israel to become more independent of U.S. aid, it will probably require that the United States consume more Israeli goods which is a degree of dependence in itself.

There are also limitations on Israel to realize substantial changes domestically. For example, the U.S. Embassy pointed out that Israel is unable to significantly reduce defense expenditures or debt repayment which account for almost two-thirds of total governmental expenditures. The prospects for achievements in reducing private consumption do not appear appreciably better. Additionally, substantial austerity measures could tempt emigration from Israel and promote labor unrest. Unless international conditions signal growth prospects, significant new investment is not likely to take place. In summation, the Embassy added that "too many of Israeli assumptions depend on circumstances either outside Israel's ability to control (i.e., world economic recovery) or beyond the bounds which Israeli democracy imposes on measures restricting private consumption."

Increasing Debt Servicing Requirements for Defense Purchases

Of the $875 million which Israel owed the United States in 1982 for debt servicing, $810 million, or 93 percent, is for defense loans. Israel has been able to cover these U.S. military debt repayments with the cash transfers it has been receiving under the ESF program. Now this situation is changing since grace periods are starting to come to an end for previous FMS loans. Thus the period of postponing Israel's defense costs is over and the impact of a large and unrealistic FMS loan program must be faced. Unless the amount of ESF is greatly increased, the difference will worsen as the decade of the 1980s continues.

To analyze the severity of Israel's debt servicing requirements, we projected the defense loan repayments coming due as compared to accounting ESF level of $785 million per year. We found that the difference between this level of ESF and the security assistance repayments will continually increase each year from $189 million in fiscal year 1983 to approximately $955 million in fiscal year 1993. Israel will face the fastest rate of increase in its security assistance repayments during this period since the termination of grace periods will accumulate.

As noted earlier, even with a general recovery of the world market for exports, it would appear doubtful that Israel can realize its optimistic forecast for export growth to help pay for this rising debt burden. Furthermore, if it were to use its foreign exchange reserves, its credit rating in the international commerical market could be adversely affected and, if it increased commerical borrowing, it would only shift the debt from the U.S. Government to the commercial market which has shorter repayment periods and higher interest terms which would heighten the overall debt in later years. Thus, Israel is more likely to make further requests that the United States assist by either increasing its economic support and/or rescheduling or forgiving prior military debts. Each of the steps, of course, would result in additional costs to the United States.

Even if the United States increased its economic assistance to maintain fiscal year 1982 purchasing power, a substantial deficit would still result. In addition, since there is a political linkage between aid to Israel and Egypt, the Congress would also have to consider the double budgetary impact of such a step. The Congress could decide to increase ESF to fully cover the debt servicing requirements as has been proposed. However, opponents of such a proposal say that the United States would run the risk of highly increased Israeli FMS requests. Additionally, Israel would thus avoid

incurring the financial impact of repaying FMS loans that calls for prudence in its spending. Furthermore, this could also set a precedent for other countries to request the same treatment. Other options for Israel include seeking more concessional loans, a greater amount of forgiveness in its FMS loan program, or further expansion of the grace period for FMS loans. Israel has already asked that the United States revert back to the one-half forgiven credits and one-half loan formula for FMS aid as was done prior to fiscal year 1981.

If the United States were to forgive more of the loans, it would have a direct effect on increasing the U.S. budget. This is because the FMS guaranteed loans are currently excluded from the need for additional budget authority and are financed through the Federal Financing Bank. We have previously reported on how this circumstance can affect the make-up of an assistance program.

In a 1977 report to the Congress, we stated that unwarranted growth of off-budget guarantees provided the potential for a poorly designed assistance program because there was potential for increased use of full guarantees where partial guarantees or more direct forms of Federal assistance are more appropriate. In a later report to the Congress, we reaffirmed this view and we also pointed out that, although it appeared likely that Israel would be able to repay current FMS obligations (mostly interest), it would encounter debt service problems when the 10-year grace periods expire and when it also begins to pay large principal payments.

A recent U.S. study on the overall balance of payments problem and debt servicing situation draws similar conclusions. The study went further than our analysis to include a projection of all debt repayment military imports in excess of U.S. military assistance, and civilian imports over exports. Given current financial policies, it concluded that **the gap in Israel's civilian imports over exports will worsen dramatically in the next few years and that, given Israel's present procurement plans, its military deficit will also grow as defense imports outstrip U.S. military aid. Additionally, it was believed that this deficit could grow substantially if the Israelis move to replace equipment lost or damaged during the Lebanon campaign. Because unilateral transfers (excluding U.S. aid) and Israeli bond sales do not normally respond to economic crises, the study concluded that a large projected financial gap will probably force the Israelis to press for additional U.S. aid or to implement austerity. However, the study concluded that Israel would only resort to a major austerity program if there were no other options. Rather, Israeli policymakers prefer to make up**

the difference through increased U.S. aid or, alternatively, commercial borrowing.
Thus, it would appear that the United States may be facing greater pressure with regards to the amounts of aid to Israel and the conditions with which it is granted.

Economic Impact of the Lebanon Crisis

According to Israeli officials, the Lebanon campaign will not result in any increase in aid requested from the United States. **However, there is a substantial foreign exchange component directly related to these activities which increases Israel's balance of payments deficit. This increase to Israel's foreign exchange needs can have an effect on its request for ESF since the request is based on an analysis of total foreign exchange needs regardless of source.**

Israel divides the costs associated with the Lebanon campaign into two categories—direct and indirect—which are to be funded over a 3-year period. Direct costs include the loss, damage to and amortization of equipment; the maintenance of reservists; and public works and transportation related to the operation. Direct costs are divided by Israel into those which can be financed domestically and those which require foreign exchange (i.e., imported goods). The indirect costs are measured in terms of the loss of production.

According to preliminary information provided by Israel, the costs are estimated as follows:

		(in millions)
Direct Costs		$1,000
Domestic component	$650	
Foreign exchange component	350	
Indirect Costs		200
TOTAL		$1,200

The $650 million direct costs are to be financed domestically over a 3-year period from budgetary cuts, an increase in the value-added tax (from 12 to 15 percent), the imposition of a 3-percent levy, a compulsory loan from wage earners and companies, and a tax on stock market transactions. **U.S. reports indicate, however, that the increased aid and better terms requested by Israel in its current aid submission include compensation for its losses during the Lebanon campaign**

The remaining 35 percent, or $350 million, represents the foreign exchange component of the direct costs which are to be financed over the next 3 years, half from private sources abroad (bond sales and the United Jewish Appeal) and half from commercial borrowing. **However, the increase of $50 million in Israel's request for FMS reflects, at least in part, aid for the replenishment of ammunition stocks drawn down and tanks lost during the fighting in Lebanon.**

The estimated $200 million in indirect costs does not include tourism losses, which, according to U.S. reports, have been substantial. For example, in June 1982, there were 22 percent fewer tourists than the year before. Using this as a basis, Israel's estimated loss in foreign revenues would be about $100 million during its fiscal year 1982. Inclusion of this component would increase Israel's total foreign exchange needs associated with the campaign to approximately $475 million (the $350 million plus the $100 million and another $25 million which Israel had already included under indirect costs for loss of exports).

Chapter 4

U.S.-Israeli Cooperative Efforts in Defense, Industrial Development and Trade

Israel is heavily dependent on U.S. financial and technical support to achieve its own arms production capability. In an effort to promote greater self-reliance, it seeks further U.S. help to assist in developing its defense industries and expand its trade opportunities.

Israel has already been granted, and continues to request additional liberalized methods and amounts of assistance beyond that of any other FMS recipient country. Among these are that Israel:

—receives trade offset arrangements from U.S. firms when it makes FMS purchases. Offsets are commitments by U.S. firms to purchase a specified amount of Israeli goods or services. Such arrangements are common under commercial arms sales but unusual under FMS;

—has asked that it be allowed to use FMS credits to purchase its own products as an integral part of the U.S. security assistance program;

—has asked that other countries be allowed to use their FMS credits to purchase Israeli goods;

—has asked that the sale of Israeli goods to U.S. armed forces be promoted and allowed without the usual restrictions placed on other countries' products; and

—has asked that the United States provide the necessary technology and funding for Israel to produce its own highly sophisticated aircraft.

Development of industrial self-sufficiency, in itself, is certainly a worthwhile goal in that less direct U.S. assistance should be needed over the longer term. However, the potential impact on the U.S. economy and employment situation, or even the U.S. ability to control the sales of advanced weaponry technology, should be considered in providing the concessions requested by Israel.

It is recognized that Israel is not currently considered a significant competitor in the international arms market but it is rapidly increasing its sales; for example, to Latin America. However, if Israeli industry and trade are eventually expanded to a point where direct U.S. assistance can be greatly decreased, the Israeli competitor factor in the international arms market will also have increased. Moreover, and possibly the most important factor for U.S. decisionmakers to consider, is the extent that the liberalized steps might be setting a costly precedent. Other FMS recipient

152

countries will most likely ask for the same. If these are granted, it will compound the long-range impact on the United States.

U.S. Commitments and Efforts to Support Israel's Defense Industry and Trade

Following the 1967 Six Day War, France placed a military embargo on Israel and it was thus spurred to become more militarily independent and to invest heavily into its defense industries. Since that time, Israel has received U.S. financial and technical support to help achieve its own arms production capability. Through domestic arms production, Israel strives to meet its own defense needs as independently as possible and maintain its qualitative edge over Arab weaponry. Nonetheless, Israel will probably remain dependent on the United States for the most advanced and sophisticated military equipment and aircraft because its production capabilities have not kept pace with worldwide technological advances.

A Master Defense Development Data Exchange Agreement with the United States (December 22, 1970) permits and facilitates the exchange of information important to the development of a full range of military systems including tanks, surveillance equipment, electronic warfare, air-to-air and air-to-surface weapons, and engineering. As of July 1982, 19 separate data exchange annexes, which cover individual projects under the agreement, had been concluded and one was under negotiation.

Israel's technological exports are heavily dependent on foreign components. Israeli officials estimate that during 1981–1982, most of their exports contained an import component of about 36 percent. In Israel's fastest growing industry, the electronics field, about 35 percent of the knowledge is acquired from the United States in licensed production or technology transfer. Almost every Israeli arms production effort includes a U.S. input, as shown in the following table (See Appendix 6).

According to a State Department official, the United States has permitted Israel to coproduce U.S. defense equipment through licensed production at a "higher level of technology" than it has any other FMS credit recipient. Part of the reason is that Israel is probably more industrialized than the other recipient countries and it has sufficient levels of FMS credits to afford high technology coproduction.

Major U.S.–Israeli defense trade agreements

A March 19, 1979, Memorandum of Agreement (MOA), and an April 1981 commitment made by former Secretary of State Haig, represent the primary basis of a Defense Trade Initiative to develop and enhance Israel's defense production and technological base. The MOA provides competitive opportunities for Israeli industry to penetrate the DOD procurement market. It permits Israeli firms to bid on certain U.S. defense contracts, without Buy American Act restrictions, and facilitates cooperation in research and development.

Secretary Haig's commitment provided for DOD purchases of up to $200 million a year to stimulate Israel's defense industry and this was made part of the Memorandum of Understanding (MOU) on Strategic Cooperation, signed on November 30, 1981. Although the commitment has been suspended, along with the MOU, its spirit and some of its initiatives continue under the 1979 MOA.

Memorandum of Agreement

The MOA is a major U.S. commitment to stimulate various types of cooperation in research and development (R&D) and procurement and logistics support of selected defense equipment. The MOA has two annexes: Annex A, which provides for three areas of cooperation in research, and Annex B, which seeks to promote reciprocal defense procurement.

Annex A

Annex A expanded the existing Data Exchange Program and provided for cooperative R&D programs. These include joint R&D; supporting R&D (one country's contractor performs R&D for the other country); equipment evaluation toward potential procurement; and competitive R&D (one country's contractor competes against the other country's contractor in bidding on contract awards). The third aspect of this annex is a Scientist and Engineer Exchange Program. This has included a tour of one U.S. scientist to Israel in 1980 and two Israeli scientists to the United States.

Annex B

Annex B provides an open-end list of over 560 military items and services on which Israeli firms can submit competitive bids on DOD requirements without application of Buy America[n] restrictions similar to the lifting of such restrictions of our NATO partners. The list was expanded from its initial 500 items and can be further enlarged. DOD can thus waive the Buy American Act with respect to Israeli products in awarding contracts for such items as parts for the M-60 and M-1 tanks; missile components; aircraft and aircraft components; and ammunition, bombs, grenades, and fuses.

Information on the level of procurement activity occurring under the MOA varies because the United States and Israel differ on what should be included. Israeli officials say that Israel is conducting about $10-15 million per year in business under Annex B, excluding a more recent $39 million contract for radios. However, Israel's figures do not include offsets or subcontracting arrangements with U.S. contractors for its major equipment purchases.

DOD has not had a formal reporting system to track subcontractor awards. One DOD official involved in the U.S.–Israeli Defense Trade Initiative estimates that, in 1981, Israeli firms sold DOD and DOD contractors between $50 million and $100 million worth of goods under the MOA. A partial list of procurement activities under the MOA (as of mid-1982) provided to us by DOD is as follows:

—DOD contract to Israel for overhaul of F-4 components ($1.7 million).

—United States leased from Israel three mine plows for evaluations of possible purchase (value unknown).

—United States leased from Israel six 105mm guns and purchased ammunition for evaluation. Further service evaluation is expected with possible buy thereafter (value unknown).

—Israeli firm won competition (joint effort) with McDonnell Douglas to sell B-300 assault weapon to U.S. Marine Corps ($11 million for fiscal year 1982).

—Israeli firm won competition to produce AN/VRC-12 radios ($39 million).

—Israel sold 9mm ammunition (value unknown).

—Israel sold tank parts for U.S. Army and FMS use ($3–$5 million).

—Israel sold pharmaceuticals to Defense Logistics Agency (value unknown).

—Israel provided ground support equipment for U.S. Air Force test. United States buy possible thereafter (value unknown).

—Israel sold conformal fuel tanks for F-15 to McDonnell Douglas (value unknown).

Defense trade initiative

After Israel extended its civil authority into the Golan Heights in December, 1981, the United States suspended the 1981 MOU and the

Defense Trade Initiative. Israel's Prime Minister also nullified it in reaction to the U.S. suspension.

The suspended Defense Trade Initiative was a DOD/State effort to enhance Israel's defense industry's competitiveness to facilitate DOD procurement of up to $200 million a year in Israeli-produced equipment. It was hoped that the initiative would ease the heavy Israeli defense burden and, ultimately, the U.S. aid burden; reduce the adverse economic effects on Israel of costly military imports; and promote both short-term improvements and long-term modernization of its defense industry. **[Deletion made but from later draft.]**

An interagency Defense Trade Task Force was established in April 1981 to implement this commitment. The Task Force sought methods for stimulating Israel's industry within existing budgetary and security assistance funding levels. It also attempted to determine market areas in which to encourage development and tried to encourage more efforts on the part of Israel's defense industries.

The loosely defined program goal provided the United States some flexibility in its implementation but there were no set procedures to handle Israeli requests. The United States, therefore, reacted to the requests on a day-to-day basis and the impact of the commitment for the defense industries and economies of both countries was uncertain.

The Task Force determined that the United States could not procure, on a competitive basis, enough Israeli military equipment to achieve the $200 million goal. It recognized that achieving or even approaching this goal would first require a mix of initiatives and efforts to enhance the competitiveness of Israel's defense industries. Some of the initiatives identified and under consideration were:

—authorizing use of FMS credits for offshore procurement on a case-by-case basis to modernize Israeli plants and equipment;

—authorizing use of FMS credits for offshore procurement of Israeli-produced equipment by Israeli defense forces and third countries;

—facilitating technical data packages/commercial data transfers;

—further expanding the list of items for DOD procurement under Annex B of the 1979 MOA;

—helping Israel create a defense marketing organization;

—developing more liberal technology transfer guidelines for Israel;

—facilitating industry-to-industry arrangements; and

—allowing Israel to sell back to the United States its obsolete and surplus equipment for possible third country transfer.

Despite the suspension of the 1981 MOU, the spirit and some activities of the Defense Trade Initiative are being implemented under the 1979 MOA. For example, the list of items for potential DOD procurement in Annex B was expanded and procurement activities continued. Israel hopes the freeze on defense trade initiatives will soon be rescinded. In its 1984 aid request, it asked for assistance to promote Israeli exports of goods and services to the United States at an annual level of $200 million as an intermediate goal. If the United States approves the request, it would assist Israel to achieve its ambitious export growth targets. **However, as noted in chapter 3, these export growth targets are overly optimistic.**

Israel wants the United States to: formally encourage major U.S. military equipment exporters to conclude buy-back arrangements with Israeli manufacturers; encourage DOD contractors to involve Israeli manufacturers as subcontractors; exercise a liberal policy with regard to reciprocal transfers of advanced technologies; and assist in the modernization of Israeli industry. Further, Israel requests permission to provide maintenance and refurbishing services to U.S. forces stationed overseas. In addition, Israel asks for further expansion of the MOA list to include non-military items, as well as facilitating such sales to the United States.

Israel's Defense Industry Exports

A large part of Israel's resources are devoted to building and maintaining its defense industry. Because of the relatively short production runs on major items of military equipment, Israel pursues an aggressive export program to help offset the large capital investments and high overhead involved in the production process.

Israel's world exports of military equipment reached $1.2 billion in 1981 (up from $400 million in 1977). Small arms, ammunition, communications and electronics, as well as obsolete military equipment, constitute the bulk of the exports. Sales and major military equipment, however, account for an increasing portion of the total.

Latin America has become Israel's prime market for military exports followed by Europe, Asia, and Africa. Sales include transport aircraft, patrol boats, antiship missiles, air-to-air missiles and substantial quantities of automatic weapons. In addition, Israel has sold 12 Kfir fighter aircraft for an estimated $196 million to Ecuador after receiving U.S. approval for third-country export of the U.S. engine used in the airplane. U.S. estimates are that this sale could open up the market for potential sales as high as

$800 million to other Latin American countries for Israel-produced aircraft if U.S. approval is provided.

In commenting on Israel's exports, a September 1982 U.S. report said: **"The demand for Israel's military equipment is growing. Israel's increased capabilities in the production of high-technology military items and the growing demand for this equipment will serve to boost foreign sales. The market for Israeli-produced equipment will be enhanced because its effectiveness in combat was demonstrated in Lebanon. The picture would brighten for Israeli military exports even more if the United States permits Third World transfers and assists the Israelis in their exports to the U.S. market."**

Encouraging Israel's Arms Industry Development of Trade Through Liberal Uses of FMS Credits

Some of the initiatives under consideration by the United States and some of Israel's own efforts to enhance its arms production base involve creative or liberal uses of FMS credits. Such uses include offshore procurement and third-country purchases of Israeli-produced end items, and requesting offsets from U.S. defense suppliers for Israeli FMS purchases of over $1 million.

While such uses of FMS credits would assist Israel's industrial base and trade, a question arises as to precedents such uses set for other FMS credit recipients. In the long term, the question becomes what is the impact of such trends on the U.S. industrial base and U.S. employment.

Requests for liberal allowances for offshore procurements

Israel is seeking to be allowed to purchase its own goods with FMS credits and to allow other recipients to use their FMS credits to make purchases in Israel as an integral part of its U.S. security assistance program. Normally FMS credits are used for purchases in the United States. Israeli officials told us that they need $150-$200 million a year in sales of their own goods, which, since they are outside the United States, are called offshore procurement. In its 1984 aid request, Israel asked that $200 million in FMS assistance be used for procurements from its industry. **While DOD is considering one of several means to help modernize Israel's defense industry, DOD remains reticent about going forward with such a commitment because of the U.S. economic situation, unemployment, and the potential precedent-setting impact on other countries' FMS requests. Additionally, there are both congressional and executive branch concerns, along**

with those in industry, over using FMS credits for offshore procurement to expand another country's arms industry.

Israeli officials told us that requests for using FMS funds for in-country production are made only if that particular item meets the following criteria:

—a high priority item which will meet a specific Israeli defense need;
—will not compete for export sales with U.S. products; and
—only limited numbers are to be produced in Israel.

Between June 1981 and June 1982, Israel proposed that it be allowed to use its FMS credits for purchases from its own industry and that other recipient countries be allowed to purchase Israeli goods with their FMS credits for the following products:

—*In-country production with Israeli FMS credits*

Merkava tank
Shafrir air-to-air missiles
Safe tank fire control systems
Lavi fighter development ($100 million over 4 years)

—*Sales to other recipient countries for their FMS credits*

Dabur patrol boats
Fouga Magister aircraft
Remote piloted vehicles
Radar systems.

In providing FMS credits to Israel's production, the United States may face future requests to subsidize the maintenance of an expanded Israeli defense industrial capability. For example, in 1977, Israel obtained permission from the United States to use $107 million of FMS funds to produce an Israeli-designed Merkava tank. The tank was considered a one-time exception by both countries. However, Israel later requested another $50 million in offshore procurement to expand its production capacity from 80 tanks to 100 tanks per year. Furthermore, Israel has asked for FMS offshore credits to build an Israeli aircraft fighter, the Lavi, citing the tank as a precedent.

In May 1982, Israeli Defense Minister Sharon requested $250 million per annum for in-country use of FMS credits for fiscal year 1983 through fiscal year 1986. He said it would be used for Merkava tank production,

Lavi aircraft development, and for other miscellaneous production. No action has been taken on this request.

Conclusions

If any FMS recipient country is granted approval to purchase its own goods as an integral part of the program, or other recipient countries are allowed to use their FMS credits to purchase goods in that country when U.S. sources are available, it could be used as a precedent for other recipients and cause an adverse impact on the U.S. economy.

Offsets: A different use of FMS assistance

The Israeli Defense Mission has a policy of requesting U.S. suppliers to offset or "buy back" from Israel goods or services equal to 25 percent of Israeli purchases of $1 million or more. Israeli officials said that this is to help offset Israel's rapidly increasing military debt repayment burden.

The Mission informed us that although this offset request has been a long-term Israeli policy, it views its success as very limited. We do not know the extent that offsets actually occurred since DOD does not review or track such arrangements.

Offsets can take the form of an arrangement where a military sale vendor promises to purchase related or unrelated goods and services from the buyer's country. These are termed indirect offsets. Offsets can also take the form of coproduction or subcontracting, where the vendor agrees to subcontract production of components or subsystems of a weapon system sale to a firm in the purchasing country. These arrangements are called direct offsets.

The use of offsets by vendors as an inducement to obtain defense sales has become more widespread and many foreign purchasers now expect to receive them as a matter of course. Offsets are ordinarily made by countries using their own funds to purchase arms without U.S. FMS assistance. More unusual are offset arrangements for procurements made with FMS credits.

The Aerospace Industries Association of America and the Electronics Industries Association conducted a survey of offset arrangements in contracts signed between 1975 and 1981. The survey, involving responses from 26 large U.S. aerospace and electronics equipment manufacturers, identified 23 countries with offset arrangements. Only four of these countries were FMS credit recipients as follows:

FMS CREDIT RECIPIENTS
WITH OFFSET ARRANGEMENTS

Recipient	Value of Offsets	Number of contracts
	($ thousands)	
Israel	262,250	12
Spain	32,400	5
Korea	5,000	1
Greece	910	1

We did not determine whether the offset agreements with Spain, Korea, and Greece were related to purchases with FMS credits. However, the survey results indicate that Israeli offsets from U.S. defense suppliers greatly exceed that of the other identified FMS credit recipients.

According to Israeli officials at the New York Mission, requesting 25 percent offsets is a long-standing policy. They said that, at any given time, some $500 million in long-term offset commitments from U.S. defense contractors to Israel are outstanding, but only about 10 percent of these offset commitments are successfully implemented. Since the U.S. government does not track offset agreements, we were unable to determine the total value of offset agreements related to procurements with FMS credits.

Indirect offset commitments generally are not firm contract commitments of purchases. Instead, the U.S. supplier agrees to use its "best efforts" to achieve certain dollar goals of purchases of Israeli goods over a specified time frame. For example, Israeli officials explained that McDonnell Douglass, in its F-15 aircraft sale to Israel, agreed to use "best efforts" to purchase $100 million of Israeli goods over a 10-year period. According to these officials, while U.S. companies may sign best effort contracts, they do not always achieve the commitments.

[Deletion made but from later draft.]

Direct offsets are those cases in which Israel asks that certain components or subsystems of a weapons system, which it is buying from a U.S. supplier, be produced in Israel. For example, as a direct offset for Israel's first F-16 aircraft purchase, an Israeli firm is producing the F-16 aircraft's composite rudder.

Often it is not economically viable for Israel to set up a capability to produce components only for its own procurement of a U.S. end item. Israeli officials told us that U.S. suppliers and the U.S. government have to be willing to accept Israel as a long-term source of supply. Only then does a proposition become economically feasible for Israel to undertake. Israel is willing to become price-competitive and obtain approval from the responsible U.S. military service for the manufacture within Israel of weapons system components for use by Israeli and U.S. forces. Israeli officials state that most Israeli firms are sufficiently competitive but it cannot do a large amount of business in direct offsets because U.S. industry is reluctant to depend on foreign sources for components.

According to Israeli officials, offset arrangements help soften the impact of massive U.S. assistance/loans on Israel's economy and reduce Israel's debt burden. These officials take the position that, since most of Israel's military aid is in the form of loans which it must pay back with interest to the United States, it needs offsets to reduce their impact. They also say that much of the offsets come back to the United States in additional Israeli purchases of raw materials and other goods. Finally, according to these officials, offsets support the long-range goal of cutting Israel's dependence on the United States and help Israel out of the "vicious cycle of borrowing to pay off debts." They acknowledge, however, that the United States could expect no change in aid levels for the short term — and that they could not estimate the amount of time that would be needed to achieve the longer term goal of self-sufficiency.

The High Price for Israel's Lavi Fighter Program

In February 1982, Israel officially decided to go forward with another indigenous fighter development program—the Lavi. Israel considers this costly program of great national importance to its high technology industrial base and military independence. However, Israel will be dependent on U.S. technology and financing for major portions of the aircraft. Israel will also be dependent on U.S. permission for third-country sales if it attempts to export the Lavi because it will have a U.S. engine. It is expected that the Lavi will be competitive with U.S. and European fighter aircraft now in existence.

The Lavi was originally intended, in 1979, to be a low cost replacement for Israel's aging A-4 aircraft. At that time, the United States supported the program in principle, and was willing to permit Israel to use its FMS credits to buy U.S. components for Lavi development. Subsequently, the Lavi's design and performance characteristics and envisioned level of technology were changed to make it more than an A-4 replacement and now the United States is reluctant to assist in its further development.

Israel, however, continues in its intent to build the Lavi and is continuing to seek large-scale U.S. financial and technical assistance for development and production. By July 1982, Israel requested authorization to obligate nearly $200 million in FMS credits in Israel for the Lavi. At the time of our review, U.S. policy on assisting Lavi development and production was under reconsideration. According to DOD, prohibiting further use of FMS funds for any aspect of the Lavi may stop the program.

Evolution of a high technology airplane

Based on discussions with U.S. industry representatives, the Lavi program concept began in 1979. Working with Israel Aircraft Industries (IAI), Israel sought to replace its aging A-4 aircraft with an indigenously designed and built aircraft. This effort would help Israel gain an additional degree of self-sufficiency, fill in the Kfir production line which was to be phased out, and keep more than 20,000 workers employed in Israel's aircraft industry. **[Deletion made but from later draft.]** Development costs at that point were estimated at $750 million and the unit "fly-away" price was estimated at $7 million, which did not include unit development costs.

By 1982, the estimated R&D costs for the Lavi program had doubled from $750 million to $1.5 billion and the estimated unit "fly-away" price had increased from $7 million to $16 million. Furthermore, Israel's rationale for the program changed to that of building its own "very advanced" aircraft. **[Deletion made but from later draft.]**

Its basis was that the United States had begun selling advanced fighter aircraft to Arab confrontation states, thus threatening to erode Israel's qualitative edge. Israeli officials identified two other reasons to continue with the program:

—Israel could maintain its technology edge and the United States would not be under pressure to sell its most advanced fighter to the Arab states since the United States had not provided it to Israel.

—Israel would have an advanced aircraft industry that would provide considerable local employment and possible export monies.

Israel seeks large-scale U.S. financial and technical aid for Lavi

In 1980, Israel had approached DOD with the program concept and obtained agreement in principle for it to coproduce the General Electric (GE) engine. At that time, the United States had no objections to Israel using available FMS credits to procure components and materials in the United States for its own use. However, the United States would not agree to using FMS credits in Israel for any portions of an aircraft which might later be sold to other countries. As requirements for a more advanced fighter changed the original design and specification, the need developed for an engine with more thrust. The Pratt and Whitney 1120 engine was decided upon.

Israel continues to request that the U.S.-authorized FMS credits be spent in Israel for its Lavi program. It requested authorization to obligate nearly $200 million in FMS credits to Israel for the Lavi engines and other components. While DOD has authorized Israel's use of FMS credits to procure the Pratt-Whitney 1120 engine, authorization for other requests were held up, pending policy decisions on the Lavi by DOD and State Department.

Israel began seeking U.S. and European companies to join as risk-sharing partners in Lavi, share in funding the R&D, and provide technical support. IAI approached major U.S. aerospace firms, but without success. U.S. industry representatives told us that IAI was asking U.S. aerospace companies to put up $300 million in risk money and work for the program. They said that IAI found that no U.S. company was willing to risk this amount on the Israeli program but that one was willing to provide information on setting up integrated logistics support and how to build aircraft prototypes.

Since U.S. manufacturers turned down Israeli requests for direct funding or risk sharing, Israel hopes to offset the development costs by subcontracting some portions of Lavi with U.S. firms and to pay for them with U.S. assistance. This was the case when Israel obtained DSAA authorization to use $181 million in FMS credits for the Pratt and Whitney engines.

The engine is still under development but is expected to be 60 to 70 percent compatible with the F-100 engine used on the . . . and F-15 aircraft. The contract provides for licensed production in Israel for about 80 percent of the engine. This contract is seen by some DOD officials as setting the precedent for permitting FMS credits to procure U.S. subcontracts for the Lavi. Israel, at the time of our review, was the only buyer for this engine.

At the time of our review, U.S. approval of contracts relating to the Lavi program were being held up pending a re-examination of U.S. policy. Three U.S. aerospace companies submitted export license applications to conduct preliminary structural design work. The competitive contract bids were valued at about $1 million each for Lavi composite wing and tail assemblies. The selected U.S. firm would be expected to continue into further phases for prototype production and ultimately final production of wing and tail assemblies. The three firms told us that Israel would expect the selected U.S. firm to phase full production into Israel. In another case, Israel also requested DSAA authorization to spend $12.3 million in FMS credits on a U.S. firm's development of flight control components for the Lavi.

U.S. policy dilemma on supporting Lavi

DOD has been operating on the Lavi policy set forth by the previous administration. According to DOD, policymakers are currently reconsidering the extent and conditions for permitting the use of FMS credits and the level of technology it is willing to release for U.S.-designed Lavi components. They consider the Lavi program an unwise use of Israeli defense funds and recognize the domestic, political, and economic repercussions of aiding a foreign country's aircraft program. We have previously reported on an analogous situation regarding Japan.

DOD policymakers also recognize that prohibiting use of FMS funds might contradict prior indications of U.S. support when FMS credits were authorized for the engine. They note that prohibiting any further use of FMS credits may stop the program as Israel probably cannot fund this effort from its own resources.

DOD had three policy options under consideration at the time of our review.

— Formalize and inform Israel of the present policy permitting the use of FMS funds only to procure components and production equipment in the United States for Israel's own use.

— Prohibit the further use of any FMS funds for the Lavi program.

— Limit the amount of FMS funds which could be used for the Lavi program based on an absolute dollar limit or a specified number of aircraft.

Conclusion

There are various steps being taken, or being considered, which would result in U.S. security assistance being used to help expand Israel's defense industry and to develop its high technology military equipment that has export potential.

At present, there is some uncertainty and a lack of definitive policy guidance regarding the degree to which the United States is willing to support such an effort. It seems appropriate to us that the many facets of the U.S. economic problems, national security interests, and the willingness of the United States to continue to support Israel's military must all be considered. Otherwise, precedents can be set to cause other recipient countries to request similar treatment, and controls over military technology might eventually be jeopardized. The potential for military exports could be expanded with U.S. assistance at a cost to the U.S. economy.

Before further concessions are granted to Israel in the defense industrial and trade areas, there might be a need for other U.S. government agencies to participate in the decisionmaking. In this regard, consideration might be given to having the Secretary of State, in full cooperation and coordination with the U.S. Trade Representative and the Secretaries of Defense, Commerce, the Treasury, Labor and other relevant . . . U.S. policy should be on the use of U.S. security assistance to develop a recipient country's defense technologies and industries which involve export potential.

Chapter 5

Peacekeeping Efforts Broaden U.S. Commitments

In accordance with the Camp David Accords, Israel withdrew from the Sinai in April 1982, after 15 years of occupation and transferred the peninsula to Egyptian sovereignty. Recognizing the financial and strategic burden of the withdrawal on Israel and the need to help Egyptian transition from reliance on Soviet weaponry, the United States extended assistance to both countries. The assistance was provided in the form of foreign military sales ($3.9 billion) and military and economic grants ($1.1 billion) over a 3-year period — $3.2 billion for Israel and $1.8 billion for Egypt. Israel has used its assistance to construct two highly-sophisticated forward combat air bases and to purchase military equipment from the United States for modernizing its defense and early warning capabilities.

The United States is also committed to continuing its participation in the peacekeeping mission in the Sinai as well as assuring Israel's security. A government-to-government agreement promises to protect Israel from treaty violations "deemed to threaten the security of Israel." If the treaty is violated, the United States will "consider" intervention through such measures as the "strengthening of U.S. presence in the area, providing of emergency supplies to Israel and the exercise of maritime rights in order to put an end to the violation."

Costly Sinai Withdrawal

As a result of the treaty, Israel relinquished an extensive military infrastructure including air and naval bases, military installations, intelligence facilities and an early warning capability. For Israel's defense forces, this meant a loss in strategic depth. The return of naval facilities limited naval operations in the Red Sea and forced redeployment to other ports. Israel also had to return the oil fields along the western coast of the Sinai and lost its civilian settlements and infrastructure.

Israel currently estimates that it will cost $5 billion to relocate its armed forces. Originally, Israel's redeployment activities were estimated to cost around $3.7 billion and take 3 years. Now Israel predicts it will take another 5 years, or until 1987, to complete the redeployment. This is because Israel has held back expenditures to lessen the impact on its construction industry and inflation rates.

U.S. Aid Defrays Israel's Redeployment Costs

The Special International Security Assistance Act of 1979 (Public Law 96–35, 93 Stat. 89) authorized $4.8 billion supplemental security assistance in support of the peace treaty. For fiscal year 1981, an additional $200 million was authorized in the Arms Export Control Act for financing additional redeployment costs. Israel received $800 million in grant aid for air-base construction in the Negev Desert and $2.5 billion in foreign military sales credits for financing the relocation of its forces. Egypt's package consisted of $300 million in economic aid and $1.5 billion in foreign military sales credits to modernize its armed forces.

In addition, the United States guaranteed a source of oil for Israel's normal domestic consumption requirements since the return of the Sinai oil fields again made it dependent on external sources. Israel is the only country that has such a bilateral agreement with the United States.

Israel has been granted a waiver, in accordance with the Arms Export Control Act and Section 42 (c), to allow it the option of using FMS credits to procure articles normally purchased under the annual FMS authorization or to purchase construction materials either in or outside of the United States.

U.S. assistance has enabled Israel to: (1) obtain two modern replacement airbases built by the U.S. Corps of Engineers with management assistance from the U.S. Air Force; (2) construct defense facilities and infrastructure in Israel; and (3) procure military articles and services for modernizing its armed forces and early warning equipment to offset the loss of the Sinai's tactical advantages. Israel is also building a third airbase with its own resources, which is to be in operation in October 1983.

As of September 1, 1982, approximately $2.3 billion or 72 percent of the special redeployment assistance available to Israel has been disbursed. The status of Israel's program is listed in Appendix 8.

Israel has held back spending the Sinai redeployment assistance, within the authorized 3 years, to lessen the impact on its economy. **In September 1982, Treasury Secretary Regan denied an Israeli request to release $713 million in a lump sum cash transfer so that Israel could place the funds in an interest bearing account to bolster its foreign exchange reserves. A Treasury official said that the Congress authorized a specified amount of assistance and that it was "not that amount, plus interest." He further stated that such a cash transfer would violate the Federal Financing Bank's policy which requires that disbursements be linked to purchases of defense articles and services.**

Use of redeployment funds

The portion of the plan funded by the FMS credit/grant assistance package comprises three parts: (1) construction in Israel by local contractors; (2) equipment purchases from the United States; and (3) the airbase construction project.

Local construction costs

More than 50 percent of the redeployment loans will be converted into Israeli shekels and spent within Israel for costs associated with relocating its Sinai forces. However, information on these expenditures was available only in the broadest context from Israel's general military construction records. The Israeli redeployment plan did note the following general areas to be constructed in the Negev for its defense forces:

--airfield infrastructure (excluding the two new airbases contructed by the United States);

—military schools and training bases;

—ground forces installations;

—communications relay systems and early warning installations;

—roads and utilities systems;

—housing facilities for military personnel; and

—logistics facilities.

Before the United States authorizes the purchase of foreign products with FMS credits, a determination is required to assure that procurements of such articles outside the United States will not result in adversely affecting the U.S. economy or industrial mobilization base. Thus, in November 1979, DSAA requested that Israel furnish the following supporting documentation for use of FMS funds to cover non-U.S. procurements:

—Identification of each relocation project for which funds are requested.

—Description of the goods and services which will be procured.

—Identification of the contractor to whom the funds will be paid.

However, this procedure was changed, according to a DSAA officials, because it would have created a paperwork burden for Israel and could have hindered the timely completion of its withdrawal from the Sinai. Thus, DSAA permitted drawdowns against the loan for in-country expenditures with documentation requirements, other than an Israeli request for reimbursement. Israel keeps receipts of all FMS offshore purchases for redeployment, but DSAA does not have a system to determine what is specifically procured with those funds converted into Israeli currency.

In January 1982, Israel did submit a report covering the use of redeployment funds converted into Israeli currency. This report advises the U.S. government of local construction and procurement expenditures during calendar years 1979 through 1981, but does not provide the specific information that DSAA originally requested in November 1979.

Procurement of equipment for Israel's modernization plan

About $900 million of redeployment aid was allocated for procuring defense articles and services to improve Israel's defense posture. Former Secretary of Defense Brown suggested types and quantities of equipment which the Israeli Defense Forces should acquire in conjunction with their ongoing modernization program. Israel agreed to all of the recommended items and other defense equipment.

Through the use of redeployment assistance funds, numerous items were added to Israel's inventory. It should be noted, however, that during 1980, a temporary change was made in the program. Israel was allowed to use these funds as necessary to fulfill its obligations under the FMS cash flow financing method. This was done until sufficient FMS funds were available to cover the obligations.

Building of highly sophisticated airbases

Relocating five squadrons of aircraft from several Sinai airfields created difficulties for Israel to comply with the Peace Treaty provisions. Construction of sophisticated replacement airbases would be an extraordinary burden on Israel's economy and construction industry and they had to be operational 'not later than April 25, 1982 (the treaty date for Israeli withdrawal). In the hope of facilitating a successful withdrawal and minimizing the economic consequences on the Israeli construction industry, the United States agreed to finance and construct two airbases.

The U.S. Corps of Engineers was assigned the role of construction agent, and assumed responsibility for executing the design and construction. The U.S. Air Force was designated the program manager with overall responsibility for the airbase program. Israel appointed its own program manager, as a counterpart to the U.S. Air Force program manager.

The original cost of the project was budgeted at $1.04 billion. As of September 1982, the U.S. Corps of Engineers had estimated a small increase to $1.07 billion. In addition to the $800 million U.S. grant, Israel had used $254 million in FMS credits to finance construction. Israeli officials estimate an even higher construction cost—$1.1 billion—which includes other Israeli costs not previously billed to the project.

The completed airbases, considered among the most modern in the world by the Corps of Engineers, met the time limit imposed by the treaty. Even though the replacement airbases were originally planned to be replications of two forward combat airfields in the Sinai, requiring only site adaptation of as-built designs, the new bases are operationally more sophisticated. Many functionally design changes were made to improve the facilities such as to provide maximum pilot and crew protection, and efficiently use minimal numbers of personnel for maintenance and operations.

The base layouts, **which include underground aircraft shelters and taxi ways,** are not comparable to any airbases the Corps of Engineers had built before. The Israeli program manager stated that these unique Israeli-designed shelters cost much more than those left in the Sinai but they offer important defense features considered critical. For example:

— **Aircraft are only exposed to attack on the runway for a few seconds prior to takeoff.**

— **Takeoff and refueling is accomplished quickly because no aircraft is blocked by another.**

In addition, many redundant and survivability aspects were built into these facilities. For example, two nearly identical warehouses were built at each base in the event that one is damaged during combat. Each warehouse has the capability to automatically sort and retrieve supplies and parts and it can be operated with a minimum of three persons. Over $10 million in redeployment aid was used to purchase the computerized systems installed at each warehouse.

Redundancy is viewed by Israeli officials as critical since they feel particularly vulnerable due to their limited number of fighter bases situated in a very small territory. The built-in redundancy, of course, raises construction costs. For example, the redundancy built into the fuel storage systems made them approximately twice as expensive.

Turnover of construction equipment and structures

Within 3 years of the treaty ratification, the two airbases were functional with the capability of operating two fighter aircraft squadrons from each base under combat conditions. A major contributing factor to meeting the treaty-imposed deadline was the use of "fast track" procedures to perform design and construction simultaneously. Much of the construction equipment, building materials and supplies was purchased before contracts and drawings were defined to speed delivery. Furthermore, new equipment was purchased rather than leasing or procuring used equipment, to preclude costly and time-consuming breakdowns due to around-the-clock usage.

The equipment did not break down as anticipated and, at the project's conclusion, one Corps of Engineer official noted that the construction equipment was generally in excellent condition. All of this equipment, as well as excess materials and supplies, was titled to Israel, in accordance with the country-to-country agreement. At the conclusion of the project, Israel either sold the items outside of Israel or transferred them to other Israeli projects. For example, approximately $1 million worth of structures, building materials and office supplies was purchased by the multinational peacekeeping organization in the Sinai. Since the United States pays for the peacekeeping force along with Egypt and Israel, this means it, in essence, repurchased part of the equipment.

A U.S. Corps of Engineers officials told us that leaving construction equipment and excess materials and supplies behind at the end of a project is not the usual practice in the United States nor in Saudi Arabia where the Corps is also involved in major building efforts. In this case, though, a prime consideration was to avoid seriously affecting the Israeli economy by selling construction equipment on the open market. Bringing the equipment back to the United States for resale was not considered economically viable because of the equipment's anticipated heavy wear.

Therefore, in accordance with the country-to-country agreement, construction equipment and building materials and supplies, amounting to $172 milllion of the contract, that remained were titled to the Government of Israel. To the extent that remaining items are of value to Israel—and this seems to have been the case in most instances—it offsets much of the additional costs that Israel incurred for the construction.

Israeli request for an increase in U.S. redeployment assistance

Considering its heavy debt-servicing, Israel has now requested that the grant portion of the redeployment assistance be increased from $800 million to an amount equal to its airbase construction costs which it estimates to be $1.1 billion. Not only is this estimate higher than the Corps' but it does not recognize that Israel was allowed to use FMS credits to fund its share rather than use its own funds as originally contemplated. Neither does it recognize that Israel gained the benefit of the leftover construction equipment and structures.

Terms of the Sinai redeployment funds may be modified in accordance with the Act, if the Congress determines that the redeployment is too heavy an economic burden for Israel. In this regard, a March 1981 U.S. report stated that the "Sinai redeployment aid from the U.S. is more than enough to cover the foreign exchange costs of the Israeli pullback from the Sinai."

Limited U.S. oversight of redeployment expenditures

Equipment purchases were processed essentially the same as under regular FMS procedures, with one exception. Every contract, regardless of amount, required prior approval under the redeployment FMS, unlike regular FMS where only contracts over $1 million require prior DSAA approval.

Regarding conversion of FMS credits into Israeli currency for local construction, where no U.S. contracts are involved, DSAA required an Israeli request for reimbursement. Repayments to local construction contractors were administered similarly to the previous offshore procurement project for Israel's Merkava tank. For redeployment, Israel proposed a "simple, streamlined" procedure, which DSAA accepted, to avoid hampering work progress. DSAA required little documentation but said that the Israelis made every effort to accurately track U.S. funds and that the applicable receipts are available for U.S. review. A major stumbling block in U.S. review of such expenditures would be the long time it would take to reconcile the high volume of transactions and the difficulty in positively determining whether they were used for redeployment.

Deepening U.S. Involvement in Peacekeeping Efforts

When Israel completed its Sinai withdrawal, U.S. involvement in Sinai peacekeeping activities rose from a 162-person civilian operation, known as the Sinai Support Mission and its overseas arm, the Sinai Field Mission, to nearly 1,260 U.S. military personnel and civilians in the Multinational Force and Observers (MFO). A major change in the focus is that the United States will no longer be the sole funding source nor the single agency monitoring movements in the Sinai.

From 1976 to 1982, the Sinai Field Mission helped assure peace in the Sinai. A key duty of that operation was to staff an early warning electronic station and monitor the approaches to strategic mountain passes. Following the peace treaty and until the Mission's termination in April 1982, the

Sinai Field Mission conducted mobile inspections over two-thirds of the Sinai.

The Protocol signed by Egypt and Israel, in participation with the United States, established the MFO on August 3, 1981. Its size is limited to not more than 2,000 infantry troops plus a coastal unit, an observer unit, an aviation element and logistics and signal units.

On April 25, 1982, the MFO assumed peacekeeping responsibilities for implementing the following provisions of the Israeli-Egyptian peace treaty (See Appendix 9):

(1) to operate checkpoints and reconnaissance patrols and observation posts along a 250-mile boundary line and within Zone C;

(2) to verify at least twice a month and upon request by either party the Treaty provisions; and

(3) to ensure freedom of navigation through the Strait of Tiran.

The 2,740-member MFO is currently comprised of contingents from 10 countries. The United States supplies the largest number of personnel and, as part of the treaty, pays for one-third of the MFO's operating costs. In accordance with P.L. 97-132, the United States must limit the total U.S. military personnel complement to a maximum of 1,200. The other developed country participants could be considered as contributing "in-kind" as they are not reimbursed for the salaries of their troops nor their regular operational expenses but, like the United States, are reimbursed for their additional costs. The developing countries (Colombia, Fiji, and Uruguay), however, are reimbursed for troop salaries and other costs according to the U.S. scale of reimbursements for participation in U.N. peacekeeping activities.

The equipment and manpower furnished by country are as follows:

(Personnel)
United States

Light infantry battalion 10 helicopters	808
Logistics support unit	356
Director General and Force Commander staff	33
Civilian observers	50

Colombia

Light infantry battalion	498

Fiji

Light infantry battalion   497

Italy

Three minesweepers   87

Australia & New Zealand

10 helicopters & crews   124

Uruguay

Transportation unit   73

France

Two small aircraft, one cargo plane plus crews   35

United Kingdom

Administrative support staff   35

The Netherlands

Signal units (81) and military police (23)   104

Force Commander's staff (73, including U.S.)   40

Total force and observers   2,740.

The United States agreed to pay 60 percent of the MFO startup costs and, thereafter, to share equally in providing the MFO operating budget with Israel and Egypt. The contribution for the first 2 years was $135 million and will be about $35 million in fiscal year 1983. Israel and Egypt paid $45 million each during the first 2 years and will pay about $35 million each in fiscal year 1983.

Indefinite U.S. Commitment

The duration of U.S. participation is open-ended, but subject to Congressional authorization and the appropriations process. In September 1981, we reported to the Chairman of the Senate Committee on Foreign Relations on the U.S. role in the Mid-East peace process. One of our concerns was that efforts should continue to eventually replace the MFO with a U.N. peacekeeping contingent. The Congress has shown similar interest, as noted in P.L. 97-132, December 29, 1981, 95 Stat. 1693, which authorized U.S. participation in the MFO. It directs the President to report annually "the results of any discussions with Egypt and Israel regarding the future of the Multinational Force and Observers and its possible reduction or elimination."

Under the terms of the 1981 protocol, both Israel and Egypt must agree to any alteration in the basic size and function of the MFO before changes occur. Moving to simpler arrangements at some point in the future would, of course, be a first step in disbanding the MFO. The former Sinai Support Mission reported that "the traditional approach to the problem of monitoring a border or a restricted area usually involves the wide-scale use of a combination of fixed observation posts and roving patrols." For this approach to be effective, which is similar to the MFO operation, a large number of people must be employed.

The Sinai Support Mission suggested in a 1980 publication, that "by using modern surveillance technology, one person located at a central monitoring facility can 'watch' a border or area that would normally require a substantial force to patrol." It suggested that the application of such concepts could make a "valuable and cost-effective contribution" to peacekeeping efforts. However, this may not be as practical for the MFO because the area being monitored is not confined to two mountain passes as was the case for the Sinai Field Mission. The cost of acquiring and monitoring sufficient amounts of surveillance equipment may mitigate against this. Further, a MFO official noted that the physical presence of military personnel, particularly U.S. forces, may serve as a better deterrent against treaty violations.

Role of U.S. troops

The battalion of U.S. troops is based at the southern tip of the Sinai near Sharm El Sheikh. The logistics support unit and the civilian observers are located in the northern Sinai near El Gorah. The U.S. contingent is responsible for staffing 10 observation posts and four checkpoints, in sectors 5 and 6 (see Appendix 9) plus a few logistics' facilities. Three platoons are rotated to the field for 24-hour watch duty, including foot and mobile patrols in proximity of the outposts.

The U.S. forces and civilians rotate on different schedules. The Americans working on the Force Commander's staff serve for 1 year, the Chief of Staff serves 2 years, and the observers serve for 1 year. The infantry troops and logistics personnel are assigned to the Sinai for 6-month periods. The rotation is not staggered, so each new U.S. contingent results in a complete turnover. Every 6 months, a battalion spends 1 month or more in training prior to its detachment and the same battalion loses about one month on its return to regular U.S. forces. This translates into 8 months of duty to complete a 6-month tour. A DOD official said that it may be more efficient to increase the tour of duty to 1 year, at least for the 356 logistic support unit personnel who are harder to replace and take longer to train. Transportation costs alone would be a substantial savings. DOD is currently considering changing the length of the MFO tour.

To deal with contingencies and in the event of an emergency, the MFO has formulated confidential standard operating procedures and rules of engagement. A DOD official states, however, that in the event of a major conflict, the responsibility of what U.S. troops will do — to stay and fight or withdraw — will ultimately be a matter for the President to decide. We were told that the U.S. battalion commander will employ standard operating procedures and rules of engagement. A DOD official stated, however, that in the event of a major conflict, the responsibility of what U.S. troops will do — to stay and fight or withdraw — will ultimately be a matter for the President to decide. We were told that the U.S. battalion commander will employ standard operating procedures as dictated by the U.S. Forces Command in contingencies involving U.S. troops. [sic]

U.S. liaison to the MFO

A need for a U.S. government focal point to handle U.S. participation in the MFO was also stated as a concern in our September 1981 report. In March 1982, the Department of State established a Multinational Force and Observers office in the Bureau of Near Eastern and South Asian Affairs (NEA/MFO) to provide liaison support. This office is more specialized and only about half the size of its predecessor, the Sinai Support Mission. Six persons are employed to prepare and justify budget requests, coordinate interagency support, provide administrative support, and recruit civilian observers.

The Congress requires annual status reports from the President on MFO activities and its associated costs for the United States. The NEA/MFO office transmitted its first report to the Congress on June 23, 1982. This report covers only a few months of operation and is basically a report on those U.S. costs associated with the MFO startup and construction related activities. According to the report, the State Department billed the MFO $98,261 for costs associated with the U.S. unit and participating personnel and for identifiable costs relating to property, support, and services provided by the United States.

Unreimbursed U.S. costs

The MFO is required to reimburse the United States for costs incurred as a result of MFO-imposed requirements. Between February and June 1982, DOD billed the MFO $3.2 million for related expenses (much more than the State Department's June 1982 report stated) but only $96,000 had been received by the United States as of September 22, 1982. The July-September bills show additional costs ranging from $1,710,600 for 12 helicopter engines to a $20 charge for painting ambulances.

Israel billed the MFO approximately $6 million for prefabricated buildings, communications equipment and life support systems. Much of this equipment was taken from the vacated air bases in the Sinai.

Sinai Field Mission equipment transferred at no cost

Although the resolution governing U.S. participation in the MFO said that all nonreimbursable U.S. costs "shall be kept to a minimum," the State Department did not bill the MFO for equipment transferred from the dismantled Sinai Field Mission. This equipment, which consisted of movable property, construction equipment and communication equipment was originally purchased for $2.6 million. According to the NEA/MFO report, a majority of this equipment "was acquired between 1976 and 1978 and it was near the end of its useful life." About 30 percent of the equipment, however, is in good to excellent condition, according to the condition codes listed on the equipment printout, and includes relatively new vehicles and unused spare parts.

The Sinai Field Mission also transferred other equipment to the U.S. Embassies in Egypt and Israel; and the base camp was turned over to the Government of Egypt in an operable condition at no cost. All of the recipients were required to pick up and transport it at their own expense, including the U.S. Embassy. According to a Sinai Field Mission report, in this way, it was able to dispose of excess equipment and phase out the Mission's operation in a rapid and efficient fashion. We were told that NEA/MFO's next report will probably state a value for the items provided without charge to the MFO from the dismantled Sinai Field Mission.

Chapter 6
Overall Considerations for U.S. Assistance

Israel's relationship with the United States, and the strong U.S. support and assistance for its defense, is founded on its staunch U.S. friendship and on its position as a democratic form of government in the Middle East region. The relationship has been supported by much of the American public and the Congress has often been willing to raise the levels of security assistance beyond the amounts requested by the executive branch. Israel has also been granted liberal concessions in the way the assistance is applied. Were these concessions not provided, additional assistance may have been requested.

As other countries in the region obtain more sophisticated weaponry, without full peaceful relations between these countries and Israel, Israel perceives that the Arabs present a greater potential threat to its existence than U.S. officials believe is present. Since the United States and the Soviet Union are the source of most of the weapons to countries in the region, either through assistance or arms sales, a growing dilemma exists for the United States as to how much assistance it can provide to maintain a proper balance between these opposing factions. Without peace, U.S. costs and arms transfers to the Middle East continue to escalate, thus complicating U.S. considerations in approving further arms sales and military assistance. For Israel, it makes it difficult for U.S. planners to mutually agree with Israel on its real military needs and how much of those needs the United States can support.

This planning effort is beginning to be further complicated because much of the assistance for Israel has been provided by the FMS program under long-term loans for which principal repayments are just now starting to come due. For Israel to be able to maintain what it considers to be adequate defense while at the same time repaying past borrowing, it most likely will need to ask the United States for financing terms even more liberal than those granted in the past.

We take no position on the level or terms of assistance to Israel but believe the precedents being set by the liberalized methods in implementing the program could be a problem if other recipient countries ask for similar concessions. A few examples of granted liberalized techniques follow:

—Israel was the first beneficiary of the cash flow method of financing which allows a country to set aside only the amount of money needed to meet the current year's cash requirement for multi-year production contracts rather than the full amount. This has allowed the countries to stretch buying power and place more orders than the available credit guarantees authorized in a given year. This implies a commitment for the Congress to approve large financing programs in future years to ensure that signed contracts are honored. Egypt and Turkey are more recent users of this technique.

—Israel has been forgiven (allowed write off) of a substantial portion of the FMS loan program ($750 million of $1.7 billion for fiscal year 1983). Now other countries have received the same benefit (Egypt and Sudan). Israel has also requested and received the forgiven portion of the FMS loans before drawing down on the interest-bearing, repayable part of the loans. This defers its interest expenses.

—Israel will receive an ESF grant totaling $785 million in fiscal year 1983, making it the largest program recipient. Funds are provided to Israel as a cash transfer, not tied to development projects as is the case for most other countries.

—Israel receives trade offset arrangements from U.S. firms when it makes FMS purchases. Offsets are commitments by U.S. firms to purchase a specified amount of Israeli goods or services. Such arrangements are common under commercial arms sales but unusual under FMS.

—Israel has been provided with military technologies having export potential. This could adversely impact on the U.S. economy and can affect U.S. ability to control proliferation of these technologies.

Israel has also asked for additional concessions to assist in further stretching its assistance. For example:

—Israel has asked that it and other FMS recipient countries be allowed to purchase Israeli goods with FMS credits. The request is pending. Normally FMS credits are used for purchase in the United States.

—Israel requested in 1982 that ESF funds be disbursed in a single payment at the beginning of the year. This would cost the U.S. Government in excess of $40 million in interest annually when compared to the usual quarterly disbursement of ESF funds. There have been no recent discussions of this matter.

—Israel is seeking to increase its annual military sales to the U.S. defense establishment to about $200 million.

—Israel is requesting more Sinai redeployment assistance although it has been provided two modern airbases, been allowed to use FMS credits for its share of the costs, and acquired the leftover construction equipment.

In deciding the structure of the military aid package to Israel, the United States is faced with considerations of Israeli policies that sometimes differ with U.S. foreign policy. As is the case of any independent and sovereign recipient, foreign assistance for Israel is not directly tied to whether it fully agrees with the United States or always acts in accordance with U.S. wishes. However, as differences arise, some elements of the U.S. public and the Government find this frustrating. Israel has used U.S.-furnished weapons in Iraq and Lebanon in a matter [sic] which, the administration has stated, may have violated the purpose for which they were provided. However, it is unlikely that U.S. officials would be willing, as a practical matter, to cut off the flow of weapons as the law provides when violations occur. Israel has also occupied areas outside its borders— Lebanon, Golan, the West Bank. U.S. policymakers question such moves but recognize Israel's fears that its enemies are otherwise too close. The costs of such actions can have an impact on Israeli requests for U.S. support.

In summary, the United States is faced with questions regarding the Israeli assistance program along with other countries that are not easily resolved. Among these are:

1. What is the impact of U.S. programs and policies on the spiraling Middle East and world arms race?

2. What are the potential impacts and increased costs to the United States if other recipients ask for and receive concessions similar to those of a precedent setting nature in the Israeli program?

3. To what extent might Israel ask for increased U.S. assistance levels and concessions to be able to repay mounting debt servicing requirements to the United States?

Agency Comments and Evaluation

Agency comments were solicited and provided by the Departments of Defense, the Treasury and State, the Central Intelligence Agency and the Agency for International Development. We appreciate the attention given to our report and the general positive nature of comments, updates and suggested changes. We have incorporated all suggested changes that bear on clarification of positions, and updating the facts of the report. In other areas, we have noted disagreements of the various positions and have presented them where they are discussed in the report.

We concur with the State Department, the Treasury and AID's assessment that U.S. financial flows to Israel remain heavily positive. Additionally, we share their concern about their need for continued separation of the ESF program and FMS repayments. Our report points out that the FMS loans and principal repayments will continue to grow. Treasury, AID and State concur. But we also point out that FMS repayments combined with factors affecting Israel's balance of payments could alter Israel's ability to pay its debt. The State Department and AID disagreed. State reported that they do not foresee the development of a severe debt situation. AID stated that there is cause for optimism about Israel's balance of payments prospects. We noted that there may be more pressure to increase assistance. We therefore have modified the report to incorporate the other view.

We concur with the State Department that this report highlights the intensive arguments of the arms situation of the Arab-Israeli dispute. Taken alone this one element of the report may present a limited perspective of the issues in this regional arms race. If one were to incorporate all of our recent reports in the area, a more detailed and pluralistic viewpoint of the arms race is presented as well as the multiplicity of other factors affecting arms decisions. Nonetheless the premise of this report is valid in that the Arab-Israeli dispute remains a major element in the increase of arms to the region.

ISRAEL

Appendix 1

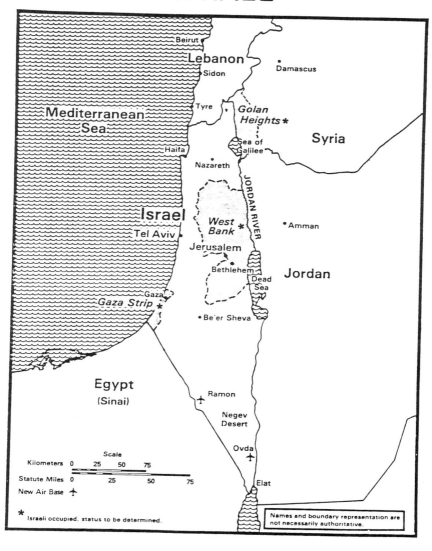

* Israeli occupied, status to be determined.

Names and boundary representation are not necessarily authoritative.

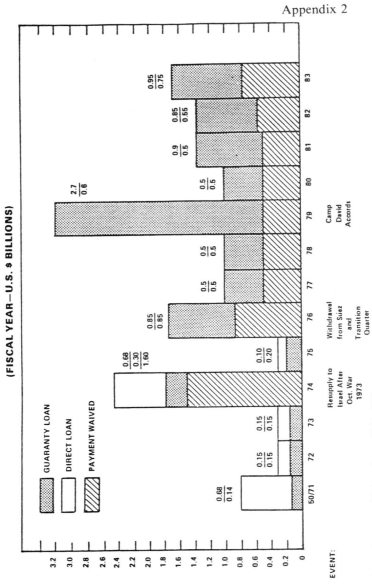

FMS LEVELS TO ISRAEL AND EVENTS DURING
INCREASES OF ASSISTANCE
(FISCAL YEAR—U.S. $ BILLIONS)

GUARANTY LOAN
DIRECT LOAN
PAYMENT WAIVED

EVENT:

Source: Department of Defense, Events added by GAO.

ISRAEL CASH FLOW PAYMENT FORECAST FOR
PROCUREMENT OF U.S. DEFENSE ARTICLES AND SERVICES

Existing cash flow obligations	Payments due			
	FY83	FY84	FY85	FY86
	($ millions)			
Purchases from DOD (FMS)	591	249	78	27
Purchases from commercial sources	440	247	78	9
Total cash flow outlay	$1,031	496	156	36

LAST THREE COLUMNS CENSORED INCLUDE TOTALS 84 / 85 / 86

Appendix 4

FY 1983 Economic Support Fund Recipient's Share of $2,661 Million

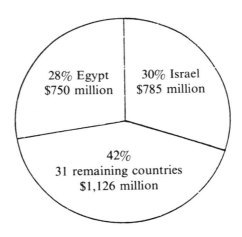

28% Egypt
$750 million

30% Israel
$785 million

42%
31 remaining countries
$1,126 million

[2] The five programs are the: Foreign Military Sales, Economic Support Fund, Military Assistance Program, International Military Education and Training Program, and the Peacekeeping Operations. The FMS and ESF programs accounted for about 93 percent of all funds related to these five programs in fiscal year 1982.

Appendix 5

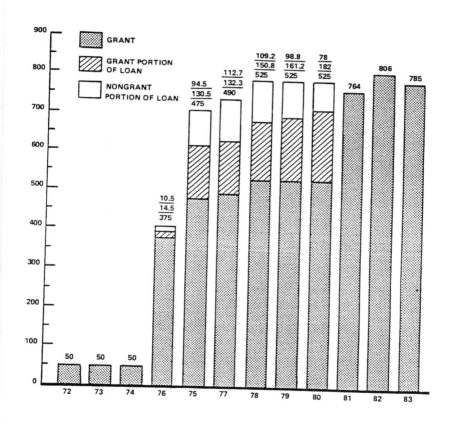

U.S. ECONOMIC ASSISTANCE FOR ISRAEL
(Disbursements in millions of dollars)

FY 1972—FY 1983
(note a)

a The loans are at a 2–3 percent interest rate with a 10-year grace period and a 30-year principal repayment term. The graph is adjusted to show the concessionality of the loans or their value in terms of a direct grant.

Appendix 6

U.S. SUPPORT FOR ISRAEL'S MILITARY INDUSTRIES

ENTIRE CHART CENSORED

	Data Exchange Agreement	Technical Data Package	Commercial Production	Commercial Procurement	Cooperative R & D	FMS Credits
Aircraft fuel tanks		x	x	x	x	x
Ammunition		x	x	x		x
Armored systems/components	x	x	x	x	x	x
Communications equipment	x	x	x	x		x
Electronic warfare/radar	x		x	x		x
Hydrofoil missile boats			x	x	x	x
Industrial equipment				x		x
Inertial systems				x	x	x
Intelligence/electronic warfare		x	x	x	x	x
jet engines/components		x	x	x		x
military engineering		x	x	x	x	x
military medicine				x	x	x
military spares and parts		x	x	x		x
precision munitions/fuses	x	x		x		x
raw materials/specialty metals			x	x	x	x
weapon delivery systems	x		x	x		x

UNCLASSIFIED   Appendix 7

Israeli Combat Fighter "KFIR C 2"

Source: Israel Aeronautics, Inc.

Appendix 8

Special Redeployment Assistance
(in millions)

Purpose	Authorized	9/01/82 Disbursed	Israel's Revised Estimate
Airbase Construction	$1,040	$1,054	$1,120
Loan	(240)	(254)[a]	
Grant	(800)	(800)	
Local Construction (Loan converted into Israeli currency)	1,254	702	2,965
Equipment Purchases	906	531	906
TOTAL	$3,200	$2,287	$4,991[b]

[a] In addition to the FMS direct loan from the special assistance package, $4.5 million was credited from a regular FMS case in April 1979 to fund start-up airbase construction costs prior to the special assistance authorization.

[b] The balance in excess of authorized U.S. aid is to be financed by Israel's own resources.

Appendix 9

MULTINATIONAL FORCE AND OBSERVERS POSITIONS

SINAI PENINSULA

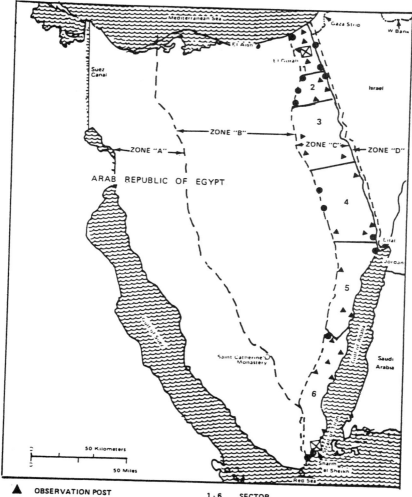

▲ OBSERVATION POST

● CHECKPOINT

1 - 6 SECTOR

⊠ MAIN BASES